WRITING ON STONE

Also by Michael Elcock

ↄ

A Perfectly Beautiful Place, Oolichan, 2004

*To Libby, with thanks for keeping
me from a wheelchair (well, almost!)
and for Paul.
With the best of good wishes
to the two of you.*

WRITING
ON STONE

Michael ❧ *Michael Elcock*

OOLICHAN BOOKS
LANTZVILLE, BRITISH COLUMBIA, CANADA
2006

Library and Archives Canada Cataloguing in Publication   .

Elcock, Michael
Writing on stone / Michael Elcock.

ISBN 0-88982-231-X

1. Elcock, Michael—Travel. 2. Scots—Canada—Biography.
3. Immigrants—Canada—Biography. 4. Scotland—Biography.

I. Title.
FC106.S3Z7 2006   971.004'91630092   C2006-902039-6

We gratefully acknowledge the financial support of the Canada Council for the Arts, the British Columbia Arts Council through the BC Ministry of Tourism, Small Business and Culture, and the Government of Canada through the Book Publishing Industry Development Program, for our publishing activities.

Cover photo: Michael Elcock

Published by
Oolichan Books
P.O. Box 10, Lantzville
British Columbia, Canada
V0R 2H0
www.oolichan.com

Printed in Canada

For Xan

You could go and work in an office,
earn money and shut out the sun,
buy cars, breathe the air air-conditioned,
and come out for two weeks for some fun.

Song: "You Can't Go On Living Forever"
—Michael Elcock

Contents

The Galloping Goose

"You go on through rolling country and soon reach, on your left, Sooke Basin and, on your right, a deep forest where you are allowed to shoot puma, as they are very plentiful..."
—CANADA, *Alaska, Saint-Pierre and Miquelon, The Bermudas,* Librairie Hachette, Paris, 1967.

This is where we live; at the edge of the deep forest, tucked into a corner of the salt-water Sooke Basin, on the southwest of Vancouver Island. In summer the woods beside our house are as rich and full with birdsong as the heath by my father's house in the south of England. Our red-winged blackbirds have a fine, inquisitive voice, as recognisable as the music of the blackbirds in Scotland. Early on spring mornings a bird sits in a tree outside the bedroom window, and serenades the new day with a lyrical, liquid song as exquisite as the music of the nightingales near Ronda in the south of Spain. Bald Eagles crowd California Turkey Vultures for space on the Pacific winds, and ride the air currents that brush the sides of Redcap Mountain.

On a summer morning, warm air pours off the rocks at the side of a cut along the old railway line, and mixes with the scent of hot, dry grass to create an aroma like burned cinnamon. The wind washes my face, warm and soft as milk, envelops me like a blanket. A young eagle, mottled brown and scruffy, is hard at work, learning how to fly. Its wings flap furiously, but they don't produce lift. The young-ster sinks steadily towards the ground, and fills the air with plaintive mewing calls. He has not yet learned how to ride the currents, how to let the winds and thermals do the work for him. The bird's mother flies to a nearby tree and watches for a few moments, then wheels out to deliver a lesson on the principles of flight. Suddenly the young bird begins to soar. Its panicked voice falls silent, and the mother watches as her youngster lifts upwards, over the Basin, higher and higher.

Tess, our brown and white Border collie, canters along beside my bike, drifts in front of the wheel, shifts to the left side. I think she's going flat out, and then a jackrabbit jumps from the brush by the old flow-line yard, and Tess jams down a gear and takes off, her body working, her head still. The rabbit runs uncertainly away from us, and then dashes into the forest. Tess is smart and edgy, always looking for something to do. My cousin from New Zealand, a farmer who's owned many dogs, says she's tractable; that she'd be a good worker if she had sheep.

On the far side of the bridge I come upon a coarse, gamey smell—stronger than deer, softer than bear. Raw and shifty like fox perhaps, but there are no foxes here. Down here the trail sprouts with wild grass, and there's not a house, nor a soul to be seen. It's how the old Sooke Road must have looked a hundred years ago, when it was travelled only on foot or on horseback. Below me the water lies flat in the

Sooke Basin, spills around the sides of Cougar Island as if it's oiled. In the distance a river of grey cloud boils down the Strait, spinning threads off its top like spume, caressing the coastline with a damp, coarse smell of sea-wrack. Above it all soar the Olympic Mountains, spired and steepled, rubbed mist-white at their tops.

This is where the Galloping Goose used to run—all the way out from Victoria, through the Sooke Hills, along beside the ocean near our house. The Goose was the name of the train that serviced the old gold fields up at Leechtown, deep in the hills. A hundred years ago thirty thousand people worked up there, sifting the shallows of the Leech River for the flash of gold. Now there's only an old man who lives there in a battered trailer. There's nothing left to show for the time of the Leechtown gold rush—except for a rusted boiler that I once came across in the woods, a hundred yards from the creek.

I was twenty-one when I set off for Canada. A Canadian girl who was studying in Aberdeen had told me about the British Columbia coast; told me stories about a young society without the social restrictions that so hampered Scotland; about Canada's raw beauty and the resourcefulness of its people; stories that were captivating and quixotic. It sounded like a place where you could do almost anything you wanted.

Emigration was the simplest way to get a work permit, and I needed to work for I had hardly any money. But I told myself that I didn't really intend to stay for long; the main idea was to travel on round the world, and make my way eventually home to Scotland. As far as Canada was concerned, I was just passing through.

But I never did go back to Scotland for good. I became an

emigrant, and like most emigrants I struggle sometimes with my place in the great scheme of things, awake from sleep sometimes straddling continents, unsure where I belong. Every emigrant lives with questions of identity. These questions can be as present as language, or as subtle as longing. For you never give up your roots, and the generations of experience that comes with them: they're part of your character and your memory, part of who you are. It can be a confusing matter when the soul is sometimes out in mid Atlantic, or mid Pacific, far from land.

Sometimes I contemplate these questions when I walk the Goose, by the sea. For every place has a past, a present and a future, which means that it turns around diverse axes, some tangible and known, some unfolding, others speculative, and mystical. Places are animated in subtle ways by people, invested with character, given layers and strata—and shape and substance which is just as fleeting as the lives that brighten them. You need to know all this to feel a place in your bones, and this can give an emigrant the most difficulty.

We built the house where we live, built it up on a rock overlooking the Basin. It took us twelve months of hard work, every evening after the office, and every weekend, and when it was done we went away to live in Scotland for two years. But we came back, and since that time we've added bits and pieces, a room here, a study there. We've taken out walls and enlarged rooms, moved a hallway somewhere else; turned a bedroom into a kitchen, cut windows in the roof to let in the sky.

I can see the United States of America from my bedroom; the Olympic Mountains in Washington State are deep violet in the evening light, beneath a dark sky splashed with streaks of red cirrus. These peaks are as high as the Alps, sharp and snow-covered in winter, green and cool in summer. In the autumn they're magnified by warm airs, so that every detail is enlarged; snowfields and crags, and even individual trees, stand out as if you could reach out and touch them. Serrated mountain ridges drift off to infinity behind, purple and grey.

The best skylight sits right over our bed, so we can watch the stars at night. People don't often get the chance to lie back and look at the night sky. We do it every night, observing the heavens through the big six-foot window above our heads. It makes me think sometimes of what it must have been like for my father during the war, when he looked through the clear cockpit glass of his bomber at the black immensity of the night, trusting the stars to help him keep his course.

Satellites spin overhead to the north and south, to the east and the west, flicking on and off like tiny pin-lights as they tumble and catch tomorrow's sun, or yesterday's. Some of these spacecraft are steady and bright, and move bullet-straight across the sky; others follow a wavy, uncertain course.

I can set my watch by the Alaska Airlines flight from SeaTac to Fairbanks. It tracks across the skylight each night at ten-thirty, like a bright, winking spider—red, green, strobe-flashing white—passing silently through the stars. The deep rumble of its powerful Pratt and Whitney engines doesn't reach our room until the aeroplane has left the frame of the glass, and moved on to the north. Sometimes, when the moon is up, the aircraft leaves a pencil-wide contrail, which drifts across the sky, feathering out white from its centre, as if a scalpel has opened a wound in the night.

At night I can tell the time by the stars, by how they

sit beside each other in the frame of the skylight, by their orientation in the great wheel of the sky, the glass above my head like the face of a celestial clock; a star-dial. When the year turns over, Orion rises out of the hills on the east side of the house, and arcs gently over the southern horizon until, at one o'clock in the morning Betelgeuse sits in the crook of the biggest of the windows at the front of the room. Alkaid moves into the skylight an hour and a half before dawn, pulling behind it a company of stars, until the Great Bear fills the glass like a picture, from edge to edge to edge, from north to south and east to west—and starts to rotate slowly out of the frame. The Greeks believed this constellation represented the beautiful Callisto, who had been changed into a bear by Hera, and later sent up to the heavens by Zeus for safety. A hundred and fifty years ago these stars were revered in song as the Big Dipper by escaping American slaves, as they made their hazardous way along the Underground Railroad to Canada. "Follow the Drinking Gourd", went the words, "to a better life in the North Countrie."

Late at night I can watch American military aircraft as they pass through the Straits to the south, winking green if they're heading out on patrol, red if they're returning to their base on Whidbey Island. There are more of these aircraft these days—though now that the Russian fishing fleets have gone I don't know what they're looking for. Maybe it's just another sign of the fear that seems to dominate that country to the south of us.

But up in this room my head lies to the east, keeping me in balance, holding the universe in equilibrium.

When we built Em's study we had to take down a big Douglas fir which had sheltered the west side of the house for years. Em spoke to it before the chainsaw started its cut, but I don't think it made any difference to the tree. We bucked it up into logs, and counted its rings. It was well over a hundred years old, a sapling when our great-grandparents were living in a different world, when their parents' parents were probably alive as well, and Victoria was Queen. We seasoned the wood for a year, and then it warmed the house for two winters, burning to grey ash in the woodstoves.

It's a good house, a lucky house, as Robert Graves might have said. We were married in it; my mother died in one of its rooms. My father saw Orion from his window one night, not long before he passed out of this world; as bright, he said, as he'd ever seen it over the desert when he was flying his bomber across Egypt, into Libya. Xan was all but born here; would have been if we'd had the courage to do it.

The house is made of cedar and fir, its foundations dowelled with metal rods into solid granite rock: a house warm and strong, with unexpected angles that give it character. Herb showed us how to build it. Herb was Em's father, a carpenter and a craftsman. He taught us how to figure out—like you might a series of chess moves—all the logical steps you have to take when you build something complex, like a house.

That was Herb's gift, teaching us to think like builders. We won't build another house; the year we built this one was hard. Besides, houses like this can tie you down, fill up with possessions; keep you close. It can be difficult, with a house like this in your head, to live in other places, other countries.

When we first came here the only thing on the property was an old cabin made of fitted cedar logs. It was April, and the scent of the arbutus trees in flower filled the air with a delicate perfume which was every bit as sweet and exotic as the fragrance that comes from the orange trees in Seville; the elegant arbutus, with its white, round flowers, and its trunk of sinewy, tan-coloured wood, that sheds its bark instead of its leaves in the fall. The cabin was small, but we fixed it up, and then we built onto it, and in the building of it, we encountered some characters. It was a time when things were not as regulated as they are now.

Dan Pederson was our first electrician. We inherited him from the man who sold us the cabin. Dan only had one eye; he'd lost the other one in a fight in the local pub. Dan was a big, powerful man, fast with his hands when he worked. But he was too often un-manned by drink, too often tardy and unreliable. It was difficult to get him to turn up with his tools and equipment, to move a task along to its next stage. But he had endearing traits. One night he came to the door at midnight, just as we were going to bed. He was three days later than he'd told us he'd be. From the breath on him, he'd come straight from the pub. But as penance he'd brought along a box full of live crabs. Dan went straight to the sink and filled a big pot with cold water, and put it on the stove. When it was boiling, he popped in the crabs. Em rustled up some sweet corn, and at one in the morning the three of us sat down to a feast. Dan never did any wiring that night, and he didn't show up again for another week.

When it was time to build the fireplace we asked around for a good granite man, and found an Italian stone-mason who lived in a tumbledown house in the hills. This was Angelo. He took me out onto his property and showed me a pile of blasted rock, and told me it was green granite. He said it would last forever. We could have as much of it as we wanted, on one condition. He wouldn't carry any of it; granite is heavy, and he had a bad back.

Angelo told me he'd been in the Italian army during the war. He'd been a cook, but he didn't like the military life. One time, he said, the *Carabinieri* arrested him and charged him with hijacking a train full of Gorgonzola cheese. Angelo was never clear about how this matter had been resolved. When I asked him, he shrugged his shoulders, and simply said, "Look at me, what would I do with a train full of Gorgonzola cheese?" At the first opportunity, Angelo said, he made his way to the British lines and turned himself in. He spent the rest of the war as a prisoner, and said he was treated well. When the war ended, he came to Canada.

Angelo turned up at the house to start work. Along with his toolbox and his lunch box he was carrying a twenty-pounder of red wine—the kind where you hook a finger in the glass loop on the neck, sling the bottle over your shoulder, and pour the wine down your throat. Em and I hauled in some bags of sand for him to mix up as mortar, and to use as a bed for the rock. After that, we carted up a day's supply of granite from the pile in the driveway, and then we went off to work. Dan's wiring had progressed to the point where the stereo was functioning, and when I drove away Angelo was rifling through my music collection.

In the evening when I came home I could hear Verdi from the top of the road, and an awful, otherworldly howling noise that sounded like an animal in pain. I ran up the stairs to the house, taking two steps at a time. The stereo was on full blast, and Angelo was kneeling in front of the fireplace, his mortaring trowel in his hand, conducting the orchestra from Milan's La Scala, and singing along with Giuseppe di Steffano at the top of his lungs—swaying back and forth, the big jug of Calona Royal Red beside him, empty, and tears coursing down his face. The red dog was lying with her jaw on the floor, an expression of exquisite pain on her face.

In West Africa, the high, January wind that blows from the Sahara Desert all the way down to the Atlantic coast of Ghana is called the Harmattan. It coats everything with fine, laterite dust, and turns the sunsets into livid works of art. In the South of France, the Sirocco that blows up from the south can be cold even in the spring—but it brings with it a breath of spice, and nudges the mind to thoughts of exotic lands. The winds around the Sooke Basin have their own character. In winter they can blow down from the Arctic, or across the mountains from the prairies. When they come from the north or the east they bring a biting cold, which freezes pipes and collects on the damp trees as hoar frost. On one ice-cold night, soon after we had built our house, I stood up on the roof and watched the northern sky dance with the wild, green flames of the Aurora Borealis.

Sometimes, after a cold snap, we'll get an ocean wind from the southwest. This wind curves up from Hawaii, passes over the cold Humboldt Current, and eventually reaches the shores of Washington State, where it caresses the Olympic Mountains before crossing the Straits. It comes in to southern Vancouver Island with force and power, accelerating downhill into a low-pressure trough, melting frost and snow so quickly that frozen pipes explode, shrivelled plants revive, and the birds start to sing again. We call it the Pineapple Express, and it always brings rain—monsoon-like rain.

Because of this strange conjunction of air and ocean currents, because of the position of the Olympic Mountains and the rain shadow they bestow upon our little piece of the Island, we live most of the time in a Mediterranean climate—a geographical freak, at forty-seven degrees north of the equator. The city of Vancouver, only a few miles to the north of us, collects the rain at the end of the Olympic's shadow; it receives twice as much rain each year as southern Vancouver Island. A traveller has to journey almost a thousand miles to the south, to northern California, before reaching the closest, true, Mediterranean climatic belt. Perhaps it's because of this that we have such an abundance of humming birds in summer; that California turkey vultures have found this place so attractive that they've begun to displace the magnificent, native bald eagles.

A quiet beach lies at the end of a winding path at the foot of our road, hidden away from all but the most inquisitive of country walkers. A kingfisher hunts there, plummets with a twitch of its tail and a flash of luminescent blue from the boughs of a cedar tree into the water, emerges with a small pilchard-like fish that the natives call oolichan. Down on Hicks's grey wharf a blue heron stands, looking for all the world like a Presbyterian minister with his hands clasped behind his long, bent back, gazing morosely into the water. Into the silence enters the swish of a raven's wings, and its rasping, throaty croak echoes around the bay as it calls for its mate.

A pair of ospreys sometimes nests down here in springtime. It's a fine thing to sit on the rocks and watch them fishing. At first when I saw them in the distance I thought they were herons, such was the span of their wings. Then, as they turned from profile to head on, I could see that their wings were slender, with a great span, like the wings of albatross. The birds circled gracefully, and then one of them dived to take a fish in its talons from the bay.

Salmon spawn in the creek which empties into the Basin here. They gather their strength, waiting until the conditions are right for them, before fighting up a series of rocky cascades to a shadowed, gravel-bottomed pool overhung with alder trees. Late one fall evening, when the sun was only a suggestion in a cloud-red sky, the red dog Grainne, relieving herself at the water's edge, was startled almost into orbit when a big, resting salmon erupted from the water beneath her rear end. Grainne ran up the beach in fright, wondering what it was that could have played such a trick at such a vulnerable moment.

Here, where the Galloping Goose line rings the waterside, Em came across a bear one day, and a few weeks later saw a dash of tawny-brown as a cougar leaped across the old rail-bed and up the bank and was gone. Last winter I caught a similar, tan-coloured glimpse of a big cat right at the limit of the car's headlights, in the half-light of evening, as I turned into our driveway.

Not long after we built the house, a little girl was taken one day by a cougar not half a mile away. A young student on a summer job at the YMCA Camp up the hill saw the big cat drag the child into the forest, and gave chase. They came to a stand off—the cougar with its jaws clamped over the little girl's head, the student screaming at it—the two of them facing one another. The student picked up a branch and hit the cougar, but the branch was rotten and it broke over the cougar's back. But the cat dropped the child and backed off a few feet, snarling and growling all the while. Then it turned and loped into the trees. The little girl was bleeding badly, and so the student ran to get help. The cougar came back and picked up the child again, but the student ran back and flung herself at the cougar again, beside herself with anger.

The cougar dropped the child and retreated, and this time the student gathered up the child and staggered away. The two of them were covered in blood when they reached the camp, but the little girl was saved.

One morning I was sitting outside eating breakfast when I heard crashing noises in the woods beside the house. Tess—who is short sighted—dashed into the forest to investigate. I peered down from the front deck, through fir and cedar and alder, to see what was making the racket. Not twenty yards away, a black bear was barging through the underbrush beside the creek, tripping through the shifting sunlight. It was a young bear, with short legs and an awkward, muscle-bound gait. Tess ran barking towards it, and the bear turned. Tess suddenly realised what she was up against, skidded to a halt and sprinted shamelessly back out of the woods. The bear continued up the creek bed towards the main road.

It was the Labour Day holiday, and it was Mediterranean dry. There was little fresh water anywhere, and the bear was probably looking for something to drink. After a while an RCMP constable turned up. He remained securely in his car.

"Fish & Wildlife are on holiday, so don't hold your breath waiting for them," said the policeman. "Dangerous wild animals should know better than to cause trouble on statutory holidays." He wound up his window and drove off.

Word about the bear went around quickly. That evening I went out to pick blackberries in the woods down the road. Dave, who lives in the last house, was digging in his garden when I heard him say, "Jeez, sounds like something out there in the woods." He ran to his front door. It occurred to me that he might have gone to get a shotgun, so I called out in case he started shooting.

The bear probably lives near here, perhaps further up the gully, maybe on the other side of the Sooke Road. It must have gone down to Veitch Creek for water, as that's the only stream around here with any flow in it at the end of summer. Towards the end of October the salmon will start running up the creek, and the bear will stuff itself full of fish for the winter. Sometime in November it will go into hibernation. We'll need rain before the salmon run, otherwise the fish will have a problem, and so will the bear when it wakes up in the spring.

Life is full here; full with the changing seasons, with preparations in the fall for winter, with plantings of vegetables and flowers in springtime for the summer. This land still contains some of the wildness that gave its native inhabitants such rich sustenance through the centuries—full with more elemental considerations than I've ever found in a city.

The Old World

White Magic

As soon as I've crossed the river, I stop to call Betty. She tells me that she has to work tonight in Aberfeldy, but Rob will meet me in the pub for supper. I turn up the music; the car leaps forward as if a bridle's been loosed. There's something about crossing the Forth Bridge—it's a gentle conversion, unspoken and known, like a kind of alchemy.

I'll be in the Highlands in an hour.

After I've checked into Tizzie's Bed & Breakfast, I wander down the lane to the Ailean Creaggan for a drink. A fellow standing at the bar has just come back to Scotland after living for twenty years in Australia. He's not sure yet if he's done the right thing. All the faces have changed, he says, and he feels out of step with the rest of the glen.

Then Rob walks in. It's good to see him again after so long. His face is still cracked with weather, and his blue eyes sparkle at his own bad jokes. We have a fine time together, with no need for concealments. His leg gives him trouble now he tells me, and he can no longer go up on the hill. The years fall away as we talk, and it doesn't seem like any time at all since I watched him striding effortlessly over the heather, high up on the old witch mountain, pointing out sheep with his crook for the dogs; eating up the tussocky ground with a rolling, giant's pace. Now he has difficulty even walking up and down the pathways of his fishing beat on the river.

Rob tells me that he put Zian down last winter. It's a sad thing. The beautiful grey Zian was a spirited young pony when we lived in Glen Lochay, dashing down his field to greet us when we went for walks, bending his long neck under the fence to nuzzle the red dog Grainne. He was always there, watching the road for passers by, part of the glen.

In the morning, Tizzie cooks me a fine breakfast of bacon and eggs, sausages and toast. I ask her to forget the black pudding. I've been away for too long; my palate has left these Scottish delicacies far behind. Tizzie's place is cluttered and untidy, but warm from the Aga range—and cosy. Children run in and out, and neighbours drop by to talk. A West African Grey parrot chatters away, punctuating its nonsense with piercing whistles. It's a homely house, with chaos never far away.

I take my leave, drive up the glen to Fearnan on the loch, and buy a Sunday paper. It's a great, windy day. Showers of rain scatter about the hills, but the air is fresh and not cold. What to do with this free day? I should make for Glen Lyon.

Glen Lyon is a magnificent, wild glen—the longest glen in Scotland. Few people go there because it's a dead end; tourists don't like turning around and retracing their steps. They don't know what they're missing. The little road winds along the floor of the glen, past tranquil farms, over-looked by high, brooding mountains.

An Crom-ghleann dubh nan Clach . . .

The dark, bent Glen of the Stones . . .

Glen Lyon is what Scotland was like when I was a boy—a place full of legends, and tales from the Fiann; an ageless place.

The road coils along beside the River Lyon, and passes under the grey and tan bulk of Stuc' an Lochan. It's nearly twenty years since I climbed to the top of the Stuc', and gazed over mountain ranges to the barren moor of Rannoch. You can see Scotland's coasts from up there, both east and west, on a clear day. Stuc' an Lochan was the site of one of the first recorded climbs in Scotland. One of the King James's went up it some time in the 1600's.

The wind is howling around the bothy at Stronuich, funnelling down the glen from the west. I cross the little bridge over the river, to make an inspection. When I camped here twenty years ago the old bothy was a ruin, with a col-lapsed roof, and black rafters pointing at the sky like broken fingers. Now someone has bought it and fixed it up, put a new roof on, and repaired the walls and windows and doors. There are curtains on the windows, bright yellow paint on the door and window frames, although no one seems to be living in it at the moment. I walk back across the bridge to the car, remembering how I spilled a pot full of stew, and burned a big, cast-iron frying pan here one night.

After our testing climb up Stuc' an Lochan, we set up camp on the soft grass beside the river. I was with half a dozen students from Edinburgh University's Outdoor Centre, and it was my turn to cook.

I built a small firepit with river stones, searched the bank for dry gorse-wood, and lit a fire. Everyone was starving hungry after the climb and the long hike back up the floor of the glen. Every few minutes one of the students came up and asked me when supper was going to be ready. The fire was eating up the wood I'd collected, so to keep them quiet I sent them up and down the riverbank to forage for more. The stewpot was bubbling away, balanced carefully on top of the stones. I tossed chopped onions and carrots in with the meat, and a packet of Bird's Eye peas.

Reaching around to put more wood on the fire, I knocked against the handle of the stewpot—and dumped the lot onto the grass. I started spooning the stew back in the pot as fast as I could, before the rich brown gravy ebbed away into the turf. I looked quickly round to see where the others were, but they were at the riverbank, busy collecting wood. When I'd returned as much of the stew as I could to the pot, I noticed that some of the peas were darker and more textured than the others, and not quite as spherical. So I peered closely at them, and it dawned on me then that some of the peas were not peas at all. Like most of the Scottish hills, our campsite was generously sown with sheep dung.

In the same second that I made this discovery, the wails of hunger from the riverbank increased in volume. "For Christ's sake is the dinner not ready yet? I'm so famished I could eat one of those scraggly sheep."

A second voice was more urgent. "Yeah, if that stew's not dished up in the next few minutes, someone'll likely be going in the river."

Another was more plaintive. "Ooh, but I can smell it from here. How long's it goin' to be? I'm ravenous!"

I tried to extract as many of the illicit peas as I could with a spoon, scooping them surreptitiously into the fire beneath the stewpot, where they flared up with a livid purple flame. I dropped the pot down closer to the fire in order to cauterise its contents as well as I could. But I could feel my own appetite diminishing as I worked away.

"God though, it smells good." I jumped as one of them came up behind me, sniffing the wind. "I've just got to have some of that stuff right now," he said, "can't wait a minute longer". He grabbed the ladle, and poured some of the stew into his bowl.

The others came running up when they saw what was happening. "Oh Jesus, that smells good!" said another. "Does that smell good or what? I'm so hungry I can't stand it. Oh yes! What did you put in it?"

We sat round the fire as the dying sun lit the tops of the mountains, and tucked into the Glen Lyon stew; everyone except me. After a few minutes one of them noticed that I wasn't eating.

"What's the matter? You not having any of it?"

"No," I replied, with as straight a face as I could manage, ". . . tummy's been a bit funny this afternoon. I might have some later." I stirred the pot, and saw that the extra heat I'd applied had charred the bottom of it badly.

"Tastes good a wee bit burned though," said one of the students thoughtfully, helping himself to more.

The frying pan was no use at all after that meal. The heat had fused the remains of the stew right into the metal. In the end, after half an hour of scraping and scouring we tossed it out into the middle of the loch.

The Bhacain stands by itself in a sheep field, far up the glen. It's mentioned in some very old writings, this strange stone, which is shaped like a dog's head. Its neck sticks out of the ground as if its body is buried underneath. Legend has it that the ancient Fiann tethered their staghounds to this stone after the hunt. In more recent times, two and three hundred years ago, the men made their women crawl under it when they came down from the high shielings at the end of summer. That way the men knew if any of the women had been with other men up there at the summer grazing—if any of the women were pregnant. The Dog Stone is still said to have a strange effect on anyone who crawls under its head.

Once I stood here in the empty glen and watched a luminous sunset:

> We are small people,
> caring for cattle,
> giving story its due,
> raising animals;
> blameless . . .
>
> dance now
> dance the best you may
>
> A river changed course
> in legend;

a dog baying
in a red sky.

Dance Now—Marilyn Bowering

Last night Rob told me that Bob Bisset died a couple of
months ago. I think of him now as I drive past his house,
and on up the winding hill road to the pass. Bob was the
local gamekeeper, a real old Highland storyteller. He always
wore the kilt; always had a greeting for passers by. I think
now of a night of his stories, when a peat fire smoked in his
hearth and the wind howled around his chimney.

Bob believed in the old traditions, and kept many of
them alive. Every spring when the snow was gone he'd hike
around the loch, and up over trackless land, deep into the
forgotten Glen Meran. He told me about an old bothy,
called Tigh nam Bodach, that stands up there, and a tradition which requires three particular stones to be placed out
on its doorstep every spring, and taken in again every autumn. Bob had been doing that for more years than he could
remember; keeping the glen safe, as people before him had
done down through the ages. As long as someone put the
stones out in spring and took them in again before winter he
said, then nothing bad would happen in Glen Lyon. Every
few years he'd go up there for a week, and cut and lay a new
thatch of rushes and marram grass for the bothy's roof.

I drive past his lonely house, and on up the hill, and
wonder who will take care of the stones now that he's gone.
I'm hoping that the gate in the high pass over to Glen Lochay will be open. It's a long way round if it's closed. I used
to have a key to that padlock when Em and I lived in the

33

glen. In recent years the forestry people have taken to leaving the gate open, although fortunately there are few tourists who know this.

The high pass between Glen Lyon and Glen Lochay is an empty, remote place. In front of his fireside, Bob told Em and me about a night he spent up there under the stars, trying to catch some men who had been poaching his deer. Bob had brought a man with him from the tiny village at Cashlie, a mile or two down the glen, but at some point in the middle of the night they both fell asleep.

They were woken up by the snorting of horses and the thumping of hooves, by the sound of metal crashing against metal. It was pitch dark and there were no stars in the sky. They couldn't see a thing. The noise kept on for long, long minutes and it seemed to come from another time and place. Bob felt the hairs standing up on the back of his neck.

Listening to him that far off winter night in the yellow light of his oil lamps, I felt a shiver as well.

I asked him how many horsemen he thought there had been.

"Not many," he said. "Maybe three or four. Possibly five. No more than that. It wasn't a big thing; not something that would have been recorded in the history books. It was just a small skirmish; maybe some wanted men, or the settling of a local score. Perhaps there was some livestock thieving at the root of it, maybe a robbery. I don't know.

"There are never any horses up there nowadays," he added quietly, "there's no grazing for them, or for cattle. Just sheep sometimes. The Blackies are the only ones that will eat the heather. But the sound the hooves made that night was

34

the noise they make on peat . . . a sort of muffled thumping that echoes in the ground as if it's hollow . . . and they were charging back and forth. I'll tell you, it frightened the life out of me."

The gate is wide open and I drive right through. There's not a soul in sight. I stop the car. Everything is just as it was when I first came to this place such a long time ago. The little lochan that Bob described is still where it was. I stare down at the patch of hill grass where the heather ends by the peaty water, and gaze at the spot where Bob said the ghostly fight took place.

At the far end of the pass, a young couple is flying a kite at the spot where the road drops down a steep hill into Glen Lochay. The red kite swoops and dives, and soars in the winds that spiral out of the conjunction of the glens. A movement catches my eye, high up on a ridge to the west, miles away: a party of climbers passing over the skyline. Then I'm driving slowly down the switchback road into Glen Lochay, thinking all the while about the time Em and I lived here.

This once was my glen.

I knew its crannies and corners.

*I tasted its winds and the colours of the wind were my colours;
fire and gold in autumn, shadow-grey in winter;*

green with life in summer.

*This once was my glen and I spoke to its moods and loved it
when rain fell, or snow, and in its sunny times.*

This once was my glen.

I knew its whisperings, its many songs. I heard the bleating of its lambs in spring: the cries of its birds.

This glen was my glen and it took from me what I had, and measured it across its mountains and hills and streams, among its trees and rocks.

And in return it gave me magic, and its magic came as a woman, and I loved her. Always.

Far down the glen, a small, broken road climbs through thin woods onto the shoulder of the old witch mountain. This old hydro road leads up the back of Creag Cailleach to a place where I used to walk the high moors to the summer shielings. One crisp winter day Em and I scared up a ptarmigan from the heather near here, and its hard croaking cries hung in the cold air like icicles. Here in springtime we would hear the mournful calls of whaups and peewits, in summer the generous, lilting songs of skylarks.

The people who lived here aeons ago were known for the quality of the weapons they made, the strength and penetration of their arrowheads, and the durability of their lance points. They made the weapons from flint and stone that they quarried from a place high up by the misty top of Craig Cailleach, Rob told us, and tribesmen would come here from all over Scotland to trade for them.

The hard stone they used to mill flour was quarried up on Craig Cailleach as well. Em and I once found a perfectly round stone mill wheel up on the ridge. It must have weighed a ton or more, and it lay on the hillside in two halves, cracked across its middle. Rob explained that the masons would make two of these millstones at a time, and chisel a hole through the middle of each one. The stoneworkers would cut a wooden shaft, and use it as an axle to fit the two stones together, so that they could run them down the hill to the valley bottom. The stone that was left up there must have broken when they were bringing it down, said Rob. No one knew, he added, how old these things were.

It's quiet up here today. It's as if I'm floating above the earth, above the trees, watching cloud shadows caress the hillsides. I can see the little cottage where we used to live, sitting at the foot of its field, white and peaceful. One day I heard a cuckoo call up here, coming from far away down the glen. It was a sound I hadn't heard since I was a child.

This is the best way to touch the soul of a place, to walk in it, and sample its spirit. Once I could walk this glen with my eyes closed and still find my way. When I left here and went back to live on the other side of the world I used to close my eyes and walk its narrow road before I went to sleep at night, seeing everything as if I were there, straining my ears for its sounds.

I leave the car by the river, and make my way down the road towards Daldravaig, past the field Rob always planted in autumn with kale; by the birch woods where Joe the Polish woodman took me to gather fuel; along the length of M's haunted field; past the track to the bridge where we made wishes on silver for ever; past the farmhouse where Rob and Betty used to live.

We lived at Tigh na Craig, a quarter of a mile down the winding road from Rob's farm, just beyond the end of Zian's field. The cottage looks the same as it was, and cattle still roam the pasture behind it, but there are no cocky bullocks today on the birch-treed mound where they used to stand. The two rowan trees at the front gate have been cut heavily back. Will they still keep the bad spirits away?

My father used to tell a story about the first time he came to visit us in this cottage. The place must have charmed him because he told the story over and over again.

He arrived from the bright lights of London on a wild, black November night, in the middle of a howling gale. The wind shook the car when I brought him here from the railway station, tried to fling us off the narrow road. The glen was coal dark, and my father couldn't see a thing except for the glow of the oil lamp in the window of our cottage. When I took him inside a log and coal fire was burning in the grate. The dog Grainne and the cat Solon were asleep on the hearth rug.

Em showed him up to the bedroom under the roof, at the top of a short, steep staircase. The ceiling sloped so sharply that my father banged his head whenever he stood up. In bed that night he fell asleep to the noise of the wind whining past the eaves, and the rain drumming against the roof a foot or two above his head, and slept the best sleep he'd had in years.

In the morning I had to take a hiking party into the mountains, and Em had to drive down to Edinburgh.

"Everything should work all right," he said I told him before I left, "but if there's no water in the tap when you go to brush your teeth, you'll have to go out the back door, cross the back garden, climb the fence under the elm tree, and walk up the field. Watch out for cow pats on the way, they'll make a right mess of your city shoes. Near the top of the field you'll find a small pool.

"This is the spring we get our water from. A pipe runs under the field from the pool, all the way down to the house. Lift the flat rock off the end of the pipe and check to see there isn't some small animal—like a mouse or a rat—stuck in there. If there is, you'll have to fish it out to clear the pipe, but there's probably a stick or something lying about that you can use."

He said I finished off the instruction with something like, " . . . and don't pay any attention to the cows in the field. They'll probably gang up and follow you, but they're just inquisitive; they shouldn't bother you."

Neil the gamekeeper used to leave us venison after a successful stalking; sometimes a slab of salmon after a day on the river. We'd find it hanging in a bag on the handle at the back door when we came home. Grainne caught rabbits and brought them proudly home, riddled as they were with parasites and fleas, frozen stiff in winter. A few days later we'd have to take the dog twenty miles to the vet at Aberfeldy for shots to deal with gastro-enteritis, or worms. In the spring, when the snow melted, the grass outside the back door was littered with white rabbit bones.

I turn away from Tigh na Craig, and walk slowly past a magnificent old Scots pine standing up by itself in a field on bunched, twisted roots, like a statue on a pedestal. I used to watch the play of light on this tree for hours, mesmerised by its range of colour and shade, thinking it as old as anything else in the glen.

☙

This was my glen all those summers ago when I lived here and breathed in its ancient stories, and loved the place.

The lopsided green shed where Joe Hapka, the Polish forester, kept his equipment stands just beyond a bump and a curve in the road. The shed is closed and padlocked now, and Joe has long been let go by the estate. Near Joe's shed, an old Black House points back centuries to a time of small-holdings and runrig farming. Then, the earthen-floored hovel was split into halves, and people shared it with cattle and sheep and chickens, all of them using the same central fire for warmth. A small sign on the freshly whitewashed wall says that the Black House is now a listed building, and open at certain times to visitors. Cleansed and cauterised.

The craggy knob of hill known as Sron a Clachan rises above this corner of the glen, dotted with silver birches. Sheep move slowly about the hillside, and the woods grow thick towards the mouth of the glen.

A group of Breadalbane Campbells rushed up here one evening in June 1646, breaking off half drunk from a christening celebration at Finlarig castle down the road. They'd heard that a raiding party of Lochaber MacDonalds was making off over the ridge with a creach of stolen cattle, and some other booty.

The Campbells caught up with the MacDonalds in a hollow called Coire nam Bonnach—the Bannock Corrie—but in the resulting fight the addled Campbells were completely overpowered. The stream that runs down the hillside from the corrie to the River Lochay has always since been known as An t-Allt Fuileach—the Bloody Burn. It ran red with the blood of the Campbells that day, when they lost more than forty dead, with another twenty critically wounded.

Rosehips are turning red beside the little sub power-station, and then I'm out onto the road which runs the length of the north side of Loch Tay. The Bridge of Lochay pub is packed with people eating Sunday dinner as I pass by its windows and walk across the hump-backed bridge, over the River Lochay.

I remember battling down this river in a kayak, blasting through stacked white water under this bridge. I'd chosen to use a Sanna, a small slalom kayak I thought too light and unstable for the students I was teaching, and when it flipped, my hips jammed in the narrow cockpit. It took me an age to extricate myself from the whirl of bubbles and black water in the deep pool beneath the bridge; so long that I thought I'd never come up.

A lane turns off at the far side of the bridge, beside Post Cottage, and I'm heading back up the glen again, on the other side of the river. How the woods are all grown up where we cut our Christmas tree! But the rest of the glen is so much the same it's hard to believe that the years have passed.

A dog barks at Boreland. Great clumps of rhododendrons surround the estate house, and stand in verdant clusters in the fields. They give the glen such fine colour in the early summer.

When the old lady died a few years ago, Rob told me, her son, the English judge, inherited the Boreland estate. All the tenants, and a number of other people from up and down the glen, gathered to pay their respects and to see her off to the next world. At the funeral, the English judge grew impatient with the slow pace of the hearse, crawling along in its Scottish way so that the walking mourners could keep up. He leaned forward in his seat and commanded the undertaker to get a move on, and the thing speeded up, causing the mourners to break into a jog, then a trot as they tried to keep up and accompany the late matriarch in the traditional manner. Eventually the hearse roared off in a cloud of dust, leaving the estate workers and villagers puffing and coughing in its wake.

Rhododendrons close in on the lane, but I can see over their tops to the soft, southern wall of the glen where the colours are painted with a gentler brush than those on the rugged north side. Silver birches trace the line of a rocky gully, which reaches up to the crest of the ridge above Tigh na Craig.

Em followed that gully up to a deserted place at the top of the ridge late in the summer of 1977, and found bones neatly set out on a flat rock on the summit. They were deer bones she said, but she couldn't imagine what fatal conjugation of circumstances had placed them so tidily where they were.

A patch of stately beech wood rises from the centre of a field in front of the river. It will be golden brown in autumn, this wood, the bark of its trees marked with beech warts—tiny growths much prized by gypsies and witches for their magic. When the leaves fall, the ground will become loud and rustling, until the damp turns the leaves into a soft, soundless carpet. The ancients used to bury their dead in beech woods, although the one I can see may have been a more recent planting.

Another ten minutes and my circuit is complete; I'm back at the place where the glen narrows above the river. A buzzard rises from the fresh ploughing by Rob's kale field, ascending on the air currents, crying like a kitten until it becomes lost in the tan and gold and bracken-brown of its backdrop.

It's good to be here. Good to see that the glen is as gentle and peaceful and full of spirits as it was when I knew it. We were its custodians once, for a short time, like the people who live here now—and the people before us down the centuries.

Glencoe

The mountain survival courses we teach at Edinburgh University's Outdoor Centre on Loch Tay are designed for students. We take them in blue vans from the shelter of Tayside, up wide Glen Dochart, and over the hills to the windswept barren of Rannoch Moor. At the far reaches of the moor we battle on foot through deep snow, onto the flank of Bheinn Bhuidhe.

Our equipment is simple and basic in order to simulate a three-day emergency in the mountains. We've brought only the bare essentials—rudimentary primus stoves and some tasteless survival rations, a change of socks and underwear, sleeping bags, collapsible shovels, ropes, crampons, ice axes, a few pitons. We haven't brought tents.

Heavy snow clouds hang over the mountaintop at the place under the summit ridge where we set up camp. It's getting dark. Eight of us are here; myself and Phil—another instructor—and six students. We split into four two-person groups and start digging. It's important in these extreme Scottish mountain conditions to stay dry and get out of the wind as quickly as possible.

It takes us two hours to dig four snowholes, each one just big enough to take two people lying close together. We build the snowholes with rounded walls, taking care to smooth off the ceiling in each one so that condensation won't drip down on us in the night. If the ceiling is smooth, all the moisture will run down to the sides of the cave, where we fashion a little ditch to carry the wetness away from the sleeping bags. At least, that's the theory.

By the time everyone has finished digging and smoothing it's dark, and starting to snow. The four caves are a dozen yards apart, dug into the side of a high snow bank in the lee of the mountaintop. We're tired, and cook a quick, unappetising supper before we crawl into our snow shelters.

Half in and half out of his hole, Phil looks up at the sky. "We should run a line out to each snowhole before we turn in," he mutters. He's been up here before. He knows you can't be too careful in these mountains in winter.

I clamber out again, and the two of us pay out the climbing ropes, knotting them together to make a continuous line, looping them around ice axes that we plant in the mouth of each snow cave.

All through the night I can hear a gale building outside my cave, howling over cornices, whistling down gullies. The storm wakes me up, and lulls me to sleep, again and again. Sometime after midnight I peer out of the entrance of my hole into a wild, spinning froth of snow-spray. The wind is shrieking over the mountainside, rising and falling in eerie cadences as if it's being driven by the voices of demented souls from antiquity. The world outside is primary, black and grey-white, seething with icy elements which could kill us in minutes.

It must have been a night like this when the Campbells attacked the MacDonalds in the glen below us, after McIain—the clan chief—had welcomed Campbell troops into his people's homes in February 1692.

Inside the snowholes we're snug and more or less comfortable, better off than we'd be with any but the most modern of Alpine tents. But despite our best efforts at sculpting, condensation drips all night from the ceiling. Two people can generate a lot of warmth in a snow cave, and their breath makes moisture; inevitably the ice begins to melt.

The King's troops burned all the crofts and drove the cattle off down the glen. The MacDonalds fled from the slaughter into the mountains. Some of them came this way in the storm, searching desperately for the doubtful shelter of the summer shielings on the Black Mount. Others climbed the peaks across Glen Etive; scrambled into secret corries behind the Buchaille, or up into the lost valley of Coire Gabhail.

Dawn soaks a flat grey light into the snowhole, and the calm, silent air that follows a spent storm. I tug on my boots, and crawl out of the narrow entrance. Everything is still, the landscape ragged and white, as if the spirits have exhausted themselves wiping the mountains clean.

The yellow nylon climbing rope we set out last night to link the snowholes, leads straight into a snow bank. The cornice above our camp must have built up in the blizzard and then collapsed and buried the other three caves.

46

The students inside them are still asleep. They're not in any danger. The holes they've dug will be intact, built as they are into older, sturdier snow inside the bank. It's when a body becomes compressed by packed avalanche snow that the danger of suffocation arises—a different kind of situation entirely.

Thirty-eight MacDonalds died by the sword and pistol in the glen below, out of a clan which numbered a hundred and fifty. But the storm accounted for many more—frightened women and children, and men who struggled barefoot into the wild night, and died of exposure and starvation.

We follow the yellow rope hand over hand, digging with shovels into the snow bank. In a few minutes we can hear snoring, then we break through to the entrance of one of the caves.

Legend says the *Fiann*, giant figures of mythology, still sleep here in this glen in caves inside the mountains, the crooning of the winds the sound of their breathing. When their leader Fingal returns and blows his hunting horn, they will waken.

Glencoe has always been a place of paradox; "the Glen of Weeping", Macaulay called it. The names that the people who lived here gave to its features were often poetic. "The anvil of the mist" was their name for a big rock on the north side of the glen; "the water of singing birds", was a spring which bubbled fresh from the ground; "the little loch of blood" a place where they had fought over the ownership of livestock.

A ski lift climbs the southern flank of Bheinn Bhuidhe, not far from where we conducted our survival course. The lift doesn't start up until mid-February; the mountains are too wild for skiing in the heart of winter. The lift only operates on weekends, there being little trade for ski areas during the Scottish work week.

Skiing conditions in Scotland are primitive by North American standards. The Glencoe lift carries skiers up to a shelf on the side of the mountain. From there, skiers have to clamber up an icy track for a quarter of a mile, to an old ski hut that the area operators euphemistically call the Day Lodge.

The Day Lodge is a clapboard shack, moored precariously to a concrete slab. It's completely unheated, except for the warmth generated by the bodies of the skiers who've jammed themselves inside. But the cramped conditions produce enough heat to melt the congealed snow that each new arrival brings in, and the floor is always inches deep in water and slush. In the course of a day this slush thickens into a breathtaking stew of half-eaten sandwiches, sweetie wrappers, spilled tea and coffee and juice, pieces of cake and biscuits and apple, bottle tops and socks.

When the wind blows, which is most of the time, the Day Lodge shakes and shivers and recoils as if it's being racked by unimaginable deliriums. There's no cafeteria up on the mountain, and no toilet except for the drifted, yellowed snow piled against the leeward wall of the old ski hut.

An old rope tow and a pomma lift drag skiers up the mountain from the hut to a small chair that runs all the way to the windblown crest of the ridge. On a rare clear day the top offers a spectacular vista of wild mountains and remote glens, as far as the Atlantic Ocean. But more often it's blanketed in heavy white cloud, and peppered with needle-sharp hail.

At the end of the day, skiers sometimes have to make their way down to the hut in whiteout conditions, scouring skis over sharp rocks. At the hut they find that their gear, which was left neatly stacked on shelves and benches, is soggy after having been turfed into the ankle-deep morass on the floor. Once everything is gathered up, a tricky slip-sliding trek follows, to the top of the lower lift, which then carries everyone down inaccessibly steep pitches to the car park at the bottom. This trip down to the valley floor at the end of the day is almost as exhausting as the journey up to the ski slope in the morning.

On one particularly wild day, the hill manager decides that the situation on the mountain has become too dangerous. A vicious storm has blown in from the Atlantic without warning, creating dangerous winter conditions, and limited visibility. Already this winter two skiers have plummeted fatally off the edge of the mountain in thick cloud, into Glen Etive. The manager shuts down the upper lifts, and starts to evacuate the mountain.

The word goes quickly round the mountain, and the exodus becomes a rush, down the hill through thickening cloud and horizontal snow, to the top of the lower lift. Skiers stand patiently in line as the chairs load up and sway off over the cliff-drop, and downward into the murk, whisking people towards the moor far below, invisible now in the blizzard. The lift ride is not an inviting prospect, but it's the only safe way off the mountain.

I'm one of the last to leave, and by the time I reach the lift the hill manager is anxious to stop it, so violently are

49

the chairs swaying in the high wind. When I'm about half way down, the whole thing stops with a whiplash jerk, leaving me swinging spectacularly, high above the ground. I can see two chairs in front of me, and one behind. The rest are swallowed up in white mist. The ground is only just visible below me, but I know where I am. I'm stuck at the highest point on the whole lift line, with the wind rising by the minute. The chair is swaying from side to side, and bouncing urgently up and down on its wire. The wind is howling like a turbine through the cable above my head, biting through my jacket and ski pants, shaking the metal lift tower below me; chilling me to my bones.

I examine my perch carefully. There's no sign of a rope, standard emergency equipment on almost every North American lift chair; no possibility therefore of shinnying down to the ground. It's much too far to jump. If I drop from here I'll be lucky to get away with two broken legs— more likely a broken neck. There's nothing to do but wait and see if the management can start the thing up again.

After an hour I'm frozen almost rigid. Then two men with a long metal ladder materialise out of the mist, and start trying to evacuate a boy and a girl from the chair in front of me. The men are having trouble positioning the ladder on the steep hillside. It takes them several attempts to connect the top of it with the front of the chair. Then the ladder pushes the chair back, comes loose, and falls all the way down to the ground. The two men fall down on top of the ladder like a pair of Keystone Cops. Eventually they manage to manoeuvre it back up into a stable position, and the skiers clamber gingerly down to the ground.

As the two men stagger up the hillside towards me, part of their difficulty becomes apparent. One of them reaches

50

inside his jacket and pulls out a metal hip flask, applies it to his mouth and takes a long draft. He wipes his mouth with the back of his hand and passes the flask to his partner.

"Hey Jimmie," the first one shouts up at me, against the gale. "Throw yer skis and sticks doon."

"I've already done that," I call back, pointing to my skis on the heathery snow below me.

"Aw. Right! Hing on then Jimmie. This could be a wee bit tricky." They stand under the chair and gaze up at me, snow and mist swirling around them.

Slowly they bring the ladder upright, as if they're landing a monster fish from the deeps.

"It's no' goin' tae reach," shouts the second one.

"Naw," calls the first, "it's goin' tae call frae some heroics right enuff." He reaches into his jacket and pulls out the hip flask again; stands swaying in the wind, and contemplates the problem, the flask half way to his mouth. It's a long ladder, but it's an even longer distance to the bottom of the chair that I'm sitting on. He takes a drag from the flask, and hands it to his mate.

"You'll jist hiv tae hing frae the chair and feel fer the ladder wi' yer feet. It'll be awright; we'll haud it steady fer you." His partner hands the flask back to him, and the first one takes another hefty belt before tucking it back in his pocket. The wind catches the ladder and the two of them nearly fall; only just manage to stop the ladder spinning from their hands.

"Can you not winch the chair up or down a few yards to a place the ladder can reach?" I'm not enthusiastic about trusting my body to the doubtful ability of these two to hold my weight on the ladder, even if I can reach it with my feet.

"No can doo Jimmie. The lift's jammed solid."

51

Turning carefully round backwards, I let myself down slowly from the chair, until I'm hanging from the waist, feeling with my feet for the top rungs of the ladder.

"Haud it steady Jimmie" shouts the first man. It occurs to me that he's shouting at his mate, not at me. I look down. The ladder is nowhere near my feet; I'm dangling over space. Slowly the two men bring the ladder back up.

"S' the wind," the second one complains, "bluddy thing's got a mindae its own."

"You'll hiv tae hing some mair!"

I let myself down until my arms are fully extended. If I can't reach the ladder now I'll never be able to pull myself back up. The top rung bangs hard against my shins, and my foot contacts the second rung. Somehow I manage to lean down and grab the top of the ladder, and slide quickly down. I can smell the whisky long before I reach the ground.

The order for the killings in Glencoe was a genuine attempt at genocide, signed by King William III in London, and delivered by the authorities in Edinburgh. It was to be an example to those Highland clans who had been tardy in declaring their allegiance to the new king.

"You are hereby ordered . . . to put all to the sword under seventy . . . You are to secure all the avenues, that no man escape . . ."

The attackers only failed to kill all the MacDonalds because they were poorly led.

Our car is covered in snow, the road out of Glencoe all but blocked by the storm. But we fire up the engine, and somehow manage to slalom past a mile of stalled cars. A cauldron of whirling snow blots out the Black Mount and Corrie Ba, where the MacDonalds used to hide the cattle they stole. We're the last people out of the glen. Later, listening to the news in front of the fire in our warm cottage in Glen Lochay, we hear that more than fifty people have been stranded overnight in Glencoe.

Encounter With The Bonxies

The train from Fort William stops right in the centre of Mallaig. It's a short walk from the station down to the ticket office on the pier. The wind is rising, flinging rain against the shop windows. The sea heaves grey in the Sound. The door of the ticket office slams itself shut behind me.

"It's a right day for that," says the girl behind the counter, gazing at my kilt. There is no one else in the office.

I look out through the window. The wind is whipping water out of the puddles on the quay. "Is the boat going to sail in this?"

The look I get is almost scornful. It tells me that they go out to sea from Mallaig in smaller boats than the MacBrayne ferry, and in much fiercer weather. But she holds her tongue in check. "You're going over for the weekend?" Her eyebrow lifts ever so slightly. "There's a ceilidh at Ardvasar on Saturday; you'll be going to that." Without waiting for an answer she asks, "Will it be a return, or are you coming back the other way?"

I think for a minute. "Just the one way will do for now," I reply, not sure what to say about the ceilidh. I hadn't known of it, but now it's a thought in my mind. I give her the money, and take the ticket that she pushes across the counter.

"You're from down south," she says laconically, not looking at me directly now. It's not a criticism, more of a question.

"Yes, from Edinburgh." I wonder if I should tell her how long I've been coming up here; that I know these hills and headlands and seaways better than most of the incomers who live now in her little town, but I decide against it. It's been two years since I was last in the homeland; it's time just to re-tune the spirit.

"Have a good trip," she says in her precise, western highlands voice. "We'll see you again when you come back through."

The wind snatches the door out of my hand, and tries to tear it from its hinges, then slams it back in my face. I lean against the door and force it open. The gale boxes me about the ears as I step out onto the pier, and whips my hair about my neck and my cheeks. I hold onto my kilt with one hand, my bag with the other. It will not do in this place to wear the kilt about my ears. Past the end of the pier the Sound of Sleat is churning, matted grey and flecked with froth. The rain is thin, but it's coming in with velocity, slanting down from dark scudding clouds, ragged as old lace at the edges, pricking exposed skin with sharp points.

Two men are standing at the foot of the gangway, as if to make sure that it doesn't blow away. They're leaning at an angle into the gale, staggering once in a while when it drops its pace and catches them out. They barely glance at my ticket as I battle my way up to them. Their eyes are red from the salt-ridden wind. One of them nods, but they don't say anything.

Upstairs in the lounge the wind buffets windows blotched with dried salt spray, and hums in the ship's wires. The sign in the small café on the upper deck suggests hot broth, but there is stew as well, and the hard, pasty Scots pies they sell at football matches.

There are not many people travelling this way today, which is just as well. The Claymore noses warily out past the stone harbour wall, and in a minute the full force of the gale hits us, and we make our way, staggering from wave to wave, across the strait to the tiny harbour at Armadale.

I can remember well the first time I came here, to this island; before the roads were widened; before armies of tourists ate up the remoteness of the place; when the idea of a bridge spanning the sea to Skye would have brought derisive laughter from the people who lived here.

I can remember the first night those years ago, that I went into the village pub. It was a spartan place of white-washed walls, with bare flagstones for a floor. There were no carpets then, but it was full of people and smoke, alive with talk. The people spoke a language I'd never heard before, and when I asked for a drink at the bar, they stopped talking. Not for long, they were more polite than that. But their eyes followed me and took me in, not with hostility, but with caution and reserve. Once I had my drink the conversations around me gradually picked up again, still in that strange language at once guttural and lyrical with its strange cadences.

It was a while before any of them spoke to me. But gradually over the days and weeks they began to include me in their conversation. Some time after that, I realised that they always spoke in English whenever I came in to the place. They were being thoughtful and polite; it was their way of trying to put me at ease.

It was a rough pub, with a rough, battered bar, and old pictures on the walls. It was a place for the local people, not designed to attract visitors. The simplicity of it mirrored the character of the people, and I grew comfortable with it. They drank whisky, these people. Drank it as if it really was what they called it—*uisge beatha*—the water of life; as if it was as vital to them as oxygen.

One day that long ago summer the pub burned down. The smoke rose up under the roof and curled out from the eaves, and the men in the fields turned to look. Some of them dropped their tools and ran towards the place. The pub was on fire! This was an event. The place was well alight when the first men reached it. The flames were already eating the rafters, and picking at the floor joists. The nearest fire engine was at Broadford, twenty miles up the road. The men soon saw that there was no point in calling up there on the telephone, and stood back to watch. It was spring, and the yellow flames were pretty against the blue Hebridean sky.

One of the men remarked that it was a shame about all the drink inside, going to waste like that. They looked at each other and wondered if some of it could perhaps be saved. A pair of them ran across the road, dived through the door, and dashed down the steps, through the smoke to the cellar. The others formed a chain. In this way they managed to extricate most of the supplies, and one or two sparse furnishings.

They piled the bottles and tins against the wall across the road, and put a tarpaulin over it to keep out the rain. Then they watched the rest of the pub burn down. The timbers were old and dry, and nothing would have put the fire out. The pub burned until the roof collapsed, and only black, smoking stone was left. Late in the afternoon, when the flames were done, the men went back to work in the fields.

The tarpaulin stayed out there all summer while Lord MacDonald rebuilt his bar. There was work in that for some of them, and it brought them extra money. The fire hadn't damaged the adjoining hotel, and there were still beds for the few travellers who came to this part of the island.

In the autumn, when it was time for the pub to re-open, Lord MacDonald and his manager went across the road and lifted the tarpaulin. They checked the bottles and crates and bags against their inventory, and all of it was there. Nothing had been touched.

The ferries brought more and more visitors across from the mainland in the years after that. Some of the visitors fell in love with the gentle way of life on the island, and stayed. Those first ones converted old crofts, and made them comfortable in a southern way, replacing peat fires with central heating, putting in fitted carpets and refrigerators. They spoke in English accents, and the language of the pub changed so that it became rare to hear the Gaelic. One or two of the incomers opened up bed and breakfast businesses.

The character of the place drew back from all this slowly and grudgingly, and as it did, more new people came to stay.

After the fire, the laird rebuilt the pub in the old way, but over the years it underwent its own conversions. These were subtle at first, but eventually carpet went down on the floor, and the stone walls were covered with sheets of wood panelling. Green-matted foxhunting pictures were hung up in brass-coloured frames, and a television set flickered staticky images above the bar. The local people hardly went there any more, and the smoky patter of voices was replaced by the sound of jukebox music.

Some of the incomers moved away after a while, disappointed with the hard winters, and with summers that produced far more rain than they'd seen when they'd first encountered the sunny beauty of the place. But others came, and boxy new houses grew up the hillside above the bay. All the coming and going made the roads busy with cars, and changed altogether the peace of the place.

Even before all these changes had taken place, Callum the Bus was growing old, so that his driving became erratic, and he was warned by the authorities that he would have to take a new driving test every year. One evening, before they eventually stopped him driving the bus up to Broadford and Portree, he came into the pub with a smile on his lean, wind-chapped face. He went to his place by the bar, and the girl put a dram of whisky down in front of him. For a long time Callum said nothing, just stared into his glass with the smile on his face.

After a while Seoris the postman said to him, "Fit's the matter Callum? Ye're neffer usually as quiet as this surely, and you've got that silly grin on your face like you've been up to something."

"Och well . . . I'll tell you about it," said Callum, pretending to be reluctant. "It all happened like this . . . I fass dri-fing this afternoon down the road to Broadford," and his voice rose and fell in its soft island way. "You know the road," he added to no one in particular. "The road to Broadford."

We all knew the road. The local people had travelled it hundreds of times. It was very narrow, and saw little traffic. Cars going in opposite directions had to back up whenever they met, until they could squeeze past each other at one of the passing places. Livestock wandered off the unfenced moors and roamed the road as well, and there were signs which read "Beware of Sheep"—an idea which greatly amused an American friend I once took up there.

"You know how I doan't like the cara-fans," Callum went on, "the ones that the too-rists come in. They take up all the road and they whill not move to one or other of the pass-sing places for the purr-pose of getting by."

We nodded. Everyone there had heard Callum ranting about tourist caravans. Another dram appeared in front of him as someone noticed that his glass was empty.

"Well, there fass a cara-fan there, near where McLeod has his croft and it had chust passed one of the pass-sing places and it would not back up. The man chust sat in his car and way-ted for me to reverse. The nerve of it! Expecting the Broadford motor bus to move over for him! Whell, I chust drove right up and stared down at him, because there wass no whay that I fass going to reverse my bus. Not for him, and not with it full of pass-engers and me being a bit late anyway for the ferrybote at Kyleakin." He took a sip of whisky, and bathed for a moment in the silence of the room. We waited patiently for him to continue.

"He wass an Englishman," he added devastatingly. "I saw it from his licence plates. He tried to back up his cara-fan but he did not know how to do it and he got himself a wee bit sideways and flustered with it all. The time was pass-ing and I fass afraid of missing the ferrybote and so I put the bus into first gear to go around him. I had two wheels up on the grass verge and it was nearly possible to get past him. But not quite. I chust caught him with my wing mirror. Chust a wee bit you know, down the side of his cara-fan." He chortled quietly to himself and his smile grew wide, and he took another sip of his dram. "Right down the side. It was quite beautiful really. Chust like a tin opener."

Callum is gone now to the great bus terminus in the sky, and there are no visitors or caravans when the ferry docks on this wild, spring day. The wind is blustery out in the Sound, but it's sheltered beside the pier, and there are wild fuchsia and woodland flowers at the side of the road. Tufts of sheep's wool hang from the fences. Offshore, Battle-ship rock sits grey and lichen-stained, and looks as if a shift-ing of the air currents could turn it into a real gunboat. It is too early in the season yet for the sprouting of camper's tents in the woods beside Ardvasar.

At the hotel Betty won't let me pay for my tea and biscuits. "Och no," she says vaguely, "I still owe you some money from last year." I can't think what she means.

Refreshed, I wander back to the pier. Donald McLean is putting in pipes to carry water to the new sailing club. Despite the cold wind he is sweating with the effort of dig-ging into the rocky soil. It is an anomaly, this sailing club. None of the islanders have sailing boats. Theirs are solid, practical working boats with oars, or tiny outboard motors, and they use them to fish lobster and sleath and mackerel, and occasionally cod and halibut. The sailing club is Ken's dream—Ken who came here after the war from England, and who is as local now as any of the natives, and much loved. Below us, Ken's boat Wallower sits at anchor in the harbour, riding the stiff wind. She's a solid little clinker-built ketch, designed to take the rolling swells of the English Channel, or the unpredictable, chopped-up waters of the North Sea. In her way she's as practical a vessel as the fishing dories of the islanders.

Seoris the postman rolls up in his red van, but he doesn't have enough room inside to give me a lift down to the Aird of Sleat, where I have to go on my way to the Point. The Aird is at the end of the paved road. It's a long way down there, about five or six miles. Beyond it, the Point of Sleat is another three or four miles over the hills. There is nothing for it but to walk.

I collect my bag from Betty at the hotel, and start off. Seoris waves as he motors past. It's a narrow, winding hilly road and the sea spreads itself out below me, sparkling like the Aegean in the spring sunshine. A ram with big curly horns stops pulling on the hill grass to register my passing; it chews insouciantly, and gazes at me with untrustworthy yellow eyes. The grass verge at the side of the road is thick with wildflowers, clubfoot, trefoil, wide-eyed susan, forget-me-not, honeysuckle.

The road drops into a small valley at Tormore, and then climbs the hill on the other side. A suspicious-looking man pops out from under a stone bridge two hundred yards in front of me, and strides up the hill, but he was probably only relieving himself. After an hour and a half, scattered white cottages hove into view at the Aird. Behind them on the hillside stands an old stone church. The day has become warm and sunny, as if the season has changed along the course of this walk from early spring to midsummer. I can hear the air humming quietly with the sounds of bees; taste a breeze warm with the scent of clover. But I know that in this place it can just as quickly turn all the way back to winter.

The paved road ends at the Aird of Sleat. Generations of island crofters have walked up here from the Point in all kinds of weather to worship at the little stone church. Beside the church, an old metal gate creaks open to a narrow track. Once I am through the gate it feels as if the ages are brushed away. I hoist my pack over my shoulder. There is nothing in front of me except the heather hills, and the winding dirt track. On either side, pools of standing water shine black and rainbow-coloured, like oil slicks among the peat.

A group of shaggy highland cattle eyes me suspiciously. They stand astride the path, and show no inclination to move. The one in the middle is a bigger, black Angus cow. As I come closer I see there is a ring in his nose. He's not a cow at all, he's a young bull and it will be difficult if he thinks that I pose a threat to his harem.

I decide to take a detour across the moor, and rejoin the track further down. There are deer on the hill above me. I count fifteen of them, dusty red, picking their way warily across the hillocks. When I reach the top of the hill I stop for a snack of bread and cheese. Below me Roger's van sits abandoned and rusting where he left it many winters ago; pushed now to one side of the track, and pirated for parts. The Sound of Sleat sparkles all the way across to the mainland, as if it is jumping with millions of silver herring.

On the far side of the Sound, the entrance to Loch Nevis is sunlit even on cloudy days. The shape of the surrounding mountains forces warm air upwards, and the temperate air dissipates the moisture above the entrance to the sea loch. This creates an unusual effect, causing the clouds to disappear, so that shafts of sunlight habitually bathe the sea in white light, and give rise to its ancient name. 'Nevis' means 'Heaven' in Gaelic.

A small group of hikers appears on the track, walking up from the Point. They're French, and they've discovered the secret sandy beach further down. I ask them if they went for a swim in the sea there, where the water is beguilingly turquoise and Mediterranean green. No, they tell me. They only sat down and drew pictures with sticks on the warm silver sand. It is probably as well that they didn't swim; despite its looks the water is stunningly, cramp-inducingly cold. The tide will wash away their tracings by nightfall.

The track passes between the hills at the side of a tumbling burn, and gives a glimpse across the sea of the scarped sea-cliffs of Rum. A gate stands at the bottom of a long hill, and a small wooden bridge crosses a stream. This place is almost completely cut off from the rest of the world. It is like a miniature fairy glen, with a deep, peat-coloured pool where we used to swim in summer. It is difficult here to even imagine the existence of cities.

Lotte's croft lies just beyond this little glen, where the land opens out into a broad corrie, with rough grazing for sheep. Lotte was an opera singer before the war in Germany, and sang with one of the top Berlin companies. She has lived here with her husband in near isolation for more than forty years now. Sometimes, when I used to come up here, I would hear her voice in the evenings, flowing out of the little glen, strong and fine in that wild place.

Georgie's house comes into view around the next corner, sitting at the head of a little bay. A pot of coffee is brewing on top of Georgie's stove. She pours out a cup right away, without asking me if I want one. She's lost weight, looks thin, younger somehow about her face and body, but older in her eyes. The twins are in bed upstairs. "They'll be pleased to see you," she says.

The twins are supposed to have the flu, but the excitement is too much for them and they fly down the stairs to say hello, then tear up and down, bringing me treasures to inspect; pieces of sheep's wool from fences, twisted sprigs of heather, strange red and green stones. Ailsa and Bitch, the two dogs, are happy to see the visitor too. They roll over side by side to have their tummies scratched.

My friend Ken's cottage sits silent and shuttered a few feet above the high tide line on the other side of the little harbour at the Point. Ken has told me to use the cottage while I'm at the Point, but Georgie doesn't have a key, and I can't find any way to get in. I turn over all the likely stones outside, and feel along the tops of windowsills and doorframes. But there is no key.

I help Georgie to settle the little girls down, and I read to them until they fall asleep; then Georgie and I talk into the night. I sleep soundly on Georgie's new carpet on the hard floor, mesmerised by the silence around me.

The sun rises early over a cone-shaped hill at the harbour entrance. Two small cairns stand on top of the hill, there to show small boats the way past dangerous rocks, and through the tricky entrance. A glassy swell shushes in and out, over seaweed and rocks.

This hill is a strange, elemental place; it feels as if it has been here, its twin cairns guiding people home, for thousands of years. It rises sharply, over two hundred feet. To landward it is steep, but on its seaward side it is almost sheer.

In all the years I've been coming here I have never climbed to its top. I decide to go there this morning.

I pick my way around the little harbour over seaweed-strewn rocks, and start climbing the cone-hill towards the cairns. The bonxies catch me high up on the steep, seaward side.

Later in the day I learn much more about the bonxie, or great skua. They roam widely out here on the west coast, dip around the tips of rocky headlands, dive over the lips of cliffs. They are unpredictable birds, and are known to attack humans, particularly during nesting season. They will press home their attacks relentlessly, and can topple people from rock faces into the sea when they take them by surprise.

They come at me out of a clear blue sky, high above the rocks. The first one brushes my hair, its claws scratching the side of my head. It comes out of nowhere, while my eyes are down confirming a foothold on the steep face. It gives me the fright of my life, and I very nearly fall. I look up, startled, to see another one tearing in soundlessly, straight at my face. There's no cover here, the rocky hill is open to the sea and the sky. I sway back against the rock and feel the wind of the skua's passing.

Flinching and feinting like a boxer dodging fists, I'm thinking right away of Alfred Hitchcock, and the suicidal, murderous birds in his film. I am completely unnerved; these birds have no fear of collision, and they come at me in silence, one after the other, peeling off like fighter planes, each one diving in steeply. As my senses sharpen I can hear the wind in their wings as they rush past. Soon they begin to screech, like avenging furies.

I dodge and weave, and pump a clenched fist up at them whenever they come close; this causes them to veer up-

wards before they hit. But I have to be wary, keep a constant
lookout for them. The birds always fly at top speed, and they
start to vary their angles, and the direction they come from.
Two of them nearly collide, coming in at me from opposite directions. They become smarter, and fly out of the sun,
planting their shadows on my face, following them in until
I can't see in the blinding light, so that I have to fend them
off by guesswork, raising my arm when I think they're near.
I nearly fall again, aware of the sea beating against the rocks
a long way below.

When I reach the top of the hill I sit down with my
back squarely against one of the loose-rock cairns, and face
away from the sun. The bonxies come at me still, brushing
the top of the cairn, inches above my head, rushing on down
towards the harbour before soaring up ready for another sor-
tie. It occurs to me that getting off the hill will be a problem;
there is no more cover on this landward side of the hill than
there was on the other. But the terrain is less severe, and I
should be able to climb down quite quickly. I start to work
out a route, and a plan. When I've rested I set off, leaping
from rock to rock like a demented Crusoe; purposely for-
saking a straight course. I'm down among the boulders at
the edge of the machair before the skuas know I've gone. It
seems to me like a magnificent escape.

Back at the cottage, the twins have decided they're well
again, and talk of taking the rowing boat out to check the
lobster pots. Georgie listens to my tale, and hands me a book
about coastal birds. 'Bonxie', I realise, is a particularly descriptive Scottish name for such an aggressive bird.

According to the writer Jim Crumley, these fierce birds
can be a real danger in nesting season, plummeting down on
unwary climbers like kamikazes. The bonxie is quite capa-

ble of dispossessing an osprey or drowning a gannet—both much larger birds.

Another writer, David Craig, suggests that the bonxie has a thinly veiled penchant for violence, even outside the breeding season. "They were not nesting yet and did not buzz us seriously, just stood on vantage points like vigilantes waiting for trouble," he wrote about one trip to the Hebrides.

I leave the Point soon after lunch, and stop at the gate on the hill above the cottage to look back. The sea is calm now, and the twins are rowing purposefully out past the cone-hill. Each of them has an oar; two tiny figures dwarfed by their landscape. As I watch them, I know that these children will be safe. They're part of the place where they live. The winds course through their thoughts; the seasons shape the things they do; the sea and the land sculpt their character.

I realise as I stand at the gate that there is a lesson here for me about territory. These wild places don't belong to everyone; they are only loaned to us by the birds and animals as we pass through—and by the people who are native to the place; people with roots through the generations. We each have different permissions to be among them, in different seasons, or for different reasons. Sometimes there is no permission at all. It is important to remember this whenever we walk the western islands by the sea.

Cauldstane Slap

Edinburgh is a city populated with ghosts. Its countenance is much the same as it was when I lived here; its buildings little changed, its back streets and side lanes—its little-known shortcuts—still there to take you around the traffic, from one part of the city to another. The city's hills are more or less the same as I knew them when I lived here, and its parks and out-of-the-way places, its views and extravagant vistas generally unchanged. It is still the city I know best, of all the cities in the world. But the people I used to know no longer walk Edinburgh's streets, and familiar houses are no longer home to friends or family. It is a city full of strangers.

The Pentland hills lie just to the south of Edinburgh, and although the boundaries of the city stretch out now to the foot of them, the hills themselves remain a relatively untouched fastness. The authorities have somehow managed to resist building roads there, and there has been little development in the confines of the hills, so that they form something of a barrier to modern travel. The result is that the Pentlands remain deliciously wild, even within sight of the city itself. It's not unusual to see that most secretive of animals, the red fox, up there, and the hills ring with the songs of moor birds—peewits and curlews—and the exquisite, lyrical skylark. Herons stand in the hill streams and wait patiently for fish, and once in a while you might see a golden eagle, or a sparrow hawk or a kestrel, sitting up on the hill winds, watching for rabbits and small vermin.

Robert Louis Stevenson used to live by the village of Swanston, just under the northern edge of these hills. In summer he'd climb up above the scree face of Caerketton, the most prominent of the tops that face the city, and sit ". . . like Jupiter upon Olympus, and look down from afar upon men's life . . ."

I'm walking along an old drove road in the hills ten miles south of the city. The road is more of a track than anything else, and a long way from any of today's main thoroughfares. To get here I've had to thread my way down a dusty farm road, past grazing sheep, and climb a sturdy gate. The old drovers followed this track for hundreds of years—and brought their cattle down it from as far back as the thirteenth century. After the industrial revolution took hold of the country and changed the face of travel, this old byway gradually fell into disuse. By the middle of the nineteenth century, the drovers had pretty well disappeared.

Soon after I've passed out of the shadow of some farm buildings, I'm enveloped completely by the hills. The track winds around tussocks and hillocks, and fords little streams, and the sun comes down hard from a clear sky. It's a hot afternoon in the middle of summer. Butterflies flit through the long grasses, and bees move among the ling heather, and make the air heavy with their buzzing. There's no wind, and as far as I can see, there's no one else out among the hills.

This ancient drove road is called the Cauldstane Slap, and I follow its winding path for two hours, until I reach its highest point and look down its far side to farmland, and the Lanark Road in the distance. Miles away to the west, a smudge of smoke suggests the city of Glasgow.

Few travellers pass this way now, but this track has been well walked over the centuries. It lies on a direct line from the Highlands to the city markets in the south, but it was used as well by lowland farmers driving stock north to the annual sales, or trysts, at Falkirk. Old people around here speak of their grandfathers telling them about the red snow which lay on this pass in late autumn; snow stained with blood from the cattle herds, their hooves worn down from walking the hard roads from the Falkirk Tryst.

In the days of the great cattle drives the farmers at either end of the Slap would try to make sure the meadow hay was cut before the cattle came—" . . . for the beasts went pretty much as they chose, and the drovers were none too careful in herding them." (Haldane, *The Drove Roads of Scotland*.)

No one now quite knows the origin of the name Cauldstane Slap, but it isn't hard even on this hot summer day to see what a harsh and unforgiving place this would be in mid winter. The word 'slap' means, in old Scots, an open gate, or a gap in a fence or a wall—in this context perhaps, a pass. Cauldstane Slap would likely have referred in that creatively expressive way of the Scots language to the ambience of the place, and particularly to the stinging, biting winds which

71

howl out of the north-west in autumn and winter, and funnel through the pass, and batter weary travellers about the cheeks and jowls.

At the top of the cut, I turn and re-trace my steps, and right away the track becomes a different road, presenting an even wilder aspect of the hills as I walk them this time from northwest to southeast. Despite the dry summer, some sections of the track are muddy, and peat black. Strange drifts of silver sand lie across the path in other places; these are probably bleached sandstone, from a wearing down of the rocks. The heather is full of bloom, displaying a range of colours all the way from deep purple to coral and white. The 'kee. . . kee. . . kee' of a buzzard floats down from the hills.

It's hot and still, and I kneel down to take a drink of cool hill water from a stream. As I straighten up, I spot a flat, bed-sized rock a hundred yards away, across the heather. The rock sits up there like a platform, offering a comfortable seat, and a lordly perch with a view over this shallow valley I'm crossing. It's difficult to reach because the heather is thick and tangled, but eventually I heave myself up on the rock. This place is gentle and timeless; the air is thick and scented. I become very aware, on this hot summer afternoon, that others have passed this way before.

The names of these hills are lowland names, rich and old, evocative in a cryptic Scots way. Seventeenth century Covenanters looking for somewhere to hold an illicit conventicle would have known the slopes of Whauplie Rig and Byrehope Mount. They'd have made a compass point from the ragged silhouette of Cloven Craig, as they crept up the Baddinsgill Burn to snatch an anxious prayer service at Wolf Craigs, out of sight of the king's dragoons. Drovers would have slept out beside their cattle in the lee of Muckle Knock, while the 'topsmen' who sometimes travelled with them stayed in relative comfort at the farmhouse down at Harper Rigg, or Wakefield.

As I sit gazing at the view, my fingers absently trace some small indentations on the rock, and I look down to see what they are. Someone has carved something here, and although the etching is old and worn, I can just make it out. It's a name—W. Hume—cut into the sandstone. Hume, or Home, is a name from the south of Scotland. The inscription is well weathered, and looks to me as if it's at least a hundred and fifty years old, probably gouged by someone using a piece of hard granite from one of the outcrops nearby.

It's not difficult then for me to conjure up an ancient companion, sitting up beside me on the rock, swinging his legs and watching his cattle graze the rough grasses, as he rests on his way south from the big tryst at Falkirk.

I wonder sometimes, as I walk Edinburgh's streets, and climb its hills and range its boundaries, what people from the past would see if they could come back here today. My grandfather would still be able to find his way to his shop. It stands where it always stood, although the people who work in it now ply a different trade. My great-grandmother would recognise her house, and deplore the property development which floods the foothills that once stretched grassy and gorse-patched from her front door. Her mother would find familiar muirs and hillsides nearer the city's centre sprouted with tenements and bungalows, their once springy turf coated with concrete and ashphalt. I'd give much then to duck behind a familiar door, and find for a few short moments that the calendar was set as it once was. But only for a minute or two, in order to re-awaken acquaintances, or re-kindle an old adventure, or perhaps in extremity to sow a seed to right a future wrong. Time so often invokes clarity.

Denholm

The station at Hassendean stands empty and deserted. A summer breeze rattles the wooden shingles, and shivers the weathered British Railways fretwork on the old buildings. Roundels of hay, dressed in sleek black polythene, are stacked between the mossy platforms, where shiny railway tracks used to run. Climbing roses, once nurtured by the stationmaster, overflow a rotting fence and tumble down the bank. Beyond the station, the round back of Minto Hill carves a slice out of the sky.

The train to Hassendean used to leave Edinburgh's Waverley station after school on a winter Friday and chug past frost-lined rail yards, its three carriages packed with schoolchildren, who would point at unmentionables flapping on washing lines, and gaze over back fences like peeping toms.

After the long climb to the watershed at Heriot, the line dropped into the valley of the Gala Water, where it stayed until it reached the mill-lined river Tweed at Galashiels. After Gala, the train rumbled along beside the slow, brown Tweed to Melrose, and its ancient, ruined abbey. Robert the Bruce's heart is supposed to be buried here, watched over by stone gargoyles of swine playing bagpipes, and other ungodly sculptures; carvings which in past times, in such a holy place, greatly upset the English.

The train sped on, past the three majestic humps of the Eildon hills, to the old market town of St. Boswells, and then curved from there across remote countryside and rolling border hills, past the tiny farmhouse hamlets of Belses and Lilliesleaf, and on to Hassendean—where my friend Ian was waiting on the platform with his father, scanning the carriages.

The hamlet of Hassendean was given a lyrical description in the Imperial Gazetteer of Scotland when it was published in 1868.

> "The surface is so gently beautiful as to have made the bosoms of tuneful poets throb, and drawn from them some of their sweetest numbers. What par excellence constitutes Hassendean, and gave name to the ancient church and the whole parish, is a winding dell . . . narrow and varied in its bottom, gurgling and mirthful in the streamlet which threads it, rapid and high in its sides . . . Near its mouth some neat cottages peep out from among its thick foliage, on the margin of its stream . . . The dell, at its mouth, comes

76

exultingly out on one of the finest landscapes of the [river] Teviot."

When we lived on the same street in Edinburgh, Ian and I saw each other every day; played football in the park at the bottom of the street, rode on the milkman's cart on Saturday mornings. Our meetings were less frequent after Ian moved away to the Borders, but we usually managed to conjure up some magic when we got together.

By the time the train left the station at Hassendean we were bucketing down that winding dell towards Denholm in Ian's father's old Ford Popular, a high-sided car which looked like a perambulator with an engine. But Ian's dad handled the car with skill, drifting round tight corners like a racing driver, brushing back bracken at the side of the lane.

We roamed the countryside around Ian's house, climbed the border hills, explored old ruins and the Stone Age fort on top of Ruberslaw, and examined the river Teviot. Ian had built a two-seater boat—a wood-ribbed construction of heavy, dope-treated, red-painted canvas—halfway between a kayak and a canoe; a clunker by today's lightweight, white-water standards, but we thought it a real river queen.

We launched the little red boat on a frost-cold morning at a spot on the river just below a weir. We were so keen to try it out that we didn't notice that the river was in spate; the water rushing past brown and threatening, moving so fast that it was tugging shrubs and bushes from the riverbank, and sweeping them off downstream. We held the gunwales against the bank, jumped in, and started paddling.

Neither of us had been in such a vessel before. The boat tipped one way, and then the other. I lost my paddle, and then the current seized us and spun us around. Suddenly it looked as if we'd be swept down the river, all the way to Jedburgh, or smashed against the stone piers of the Denholm bridge. We both grabbed the branches of a willow tree as we shot past, and the boat flipped, and dumped us in the icy water.

That close to the bank it was just shallow enough for us to find our feet. We staggered ashore, dragging the waterlogged boat behind us. We emptied out the water and set off, wet and shivering, up the path to the bridge. One of the local worthies was leaning on the parapet of the bridge as we trudged past. "A fine pair o' captains you are," he said.

The Earl of Douglas granted much of the church land around Denholm and Hassendean to the monks of Melrose in the middle of the fourteenth century. Among the properties the monks were given was the farm at Honeyburn, and the farmhouse still has a cross on its gable end. Here, the monks are said to have had an extensive apiary, which supplied them with honey.

Warned to keep away from the river, and oblivious to the spiritual antecedents of the area, we built a hideaway in a barn near Honeyburn, at the far end of the haugh, the low-lying land beside the river. This was an ambitious construction, and it soon became an intricate series of hideouts and inter-connecting tunnels, deep inside the hay. We built complicated escape routes to spirit us out of the barn if the farmer, or any of his workers, turned up. The best of these exits took us up a tunnel in the hay to a place under the roof. From there we could swing twenty feet on a rope, down to the roof of a cattle byre, and jump onto a pile of loose hay on the ground—although one day the farmer replaced the hay with a foul pile of silage.

The project ended in disaster when the farmer—a bad-tempered, florid-faced man—inadvertently found one of the emergency entrances to this warren of tunnels when he was standing on top of the mountain of hay. Farmer Galloway discovered one of our 'crash dive' shafts; a vertical pipe we had excavated into the hay for use in an emergency—a shaft just wide enough to admit a body. This hole fell straight down for twenty feet, and dumped Galloway into a tiny cell, in total darkness and complete silence, somewhere deep in the middle of tons of winter hay. Ian and I had practised our emergencies frequently, and we'd learned to break our fall on the way down, and what to expect at the bottom. And every time we left the barn, we covered the hole with a layer of straw to make sure it wasn't detected.

We heard the story of the farmer's fateful incident quite quickly. According to the farm's tractor man, Mr. Galloway was standing on top of the hay, heaving bales down to the trailer one second, and the next second he'd vanished. The tractor man had no idea where his boss had gone.

"Ah thocht he'd gone awa' doon the back somehow, tae see the missus, ken?" the tractor man said later in the bar at the Cross Keys.

From the farmer's point of view the solid bales beneath his feet just opened up and swallowed him. The wind was knocked out of him when he crashed into the pitch-black little room at the bottom of the shaft after his twenty-foot free fall.

We had constructed two exit tunnels out of that little room. They went through the hay to opposite sides of the barn, and gave us a choice of departure, depending on where the danger was coming from. But these tunnels were difficult to find in the dark, and the farmer didn't know about them.

After sitting down there for a while getting his breath back, Mr. Galloway also discovered that it was impossible for him to climb back up the narrow chute that he'd fallen down.

The tractor man got tired of waiting for his boss to re-appear, and went home for his supper. It was more than an hour before the farmer's wife went out to the barn and heard her husband's muffled cries for help. She immediately called out the tractor man and another of the farm workers. The three of them searched inside the barn, and the byre next door, trying to figure out where the strange noises were com-ing from. In the end they realised that they must be coming from somewhere inside the hay.

The farm workers had to remove most of the bales before they found farmer Galloway. This took them a long time, because it was a big barn, and it was stacked thirty feet high with hay, almost to its roof. They didn't finish until after dark, working away in the headlights of the tractor. By the time they found the farmer, the barn was virtually empty, with all the bales out in the farmyard. It was raining by then, and they had to put all the hay back inside again before they could go home.

A breath of wind brings the soft scent of wild roses. Cloud shadows skim the face of Minto Hill. A stray piece of poly-thene flaps against a broken paling on the station fence, and sounds for a second like a distant train clattering over points. Beyond the plastic-wrapped hay the line of the track, over-grown with brambles and small trees, stretches up the valley towards the old market town of Hawick.

Despite its lovely setting, Hassendean has known its share of trouble. After the upheavals of the Reformation in the seventeenth century, Scotland went through fifty years of social unrest and religious persecution. It was a complicated period, and its reverberations are still felt down the centuries. Presbyterianism was outlawed by royal decree, but few Scots were prepared to accept the King of England as head of the church—much less the imposition of an English form of worship. In 1661, Charles II appointed bishops and curates to govern the Scottish churches, and expelled hundreds of 'non-conforming' ministers.

Faced with the loss of their churches, and with informers who would report illegal worship to the authorities, the Scots took to the hills, and held secret conventicles all across south and central Scotland. By 1670, attendance at these was deemed to be treasonable, and punishable by death. Landowners who failed to report the conventicles lost their land. Cruelty and slaughter followed; it was a time when families were hanged from the lintels of their front doors, when soldiers marked old men with branding irons, and entertained themselves by throwing women into pits of snakes.

In Hassendean, the church and its lands were given to the Earl of Buccleuch. But the parishioners resisted all efforts at religious suppression. Things came to a head here in 1690, when the authorities took the roof off the church, and set about trying to demolish the whole structure.

The first workman to set foot on a ladder to start the demolition is said to have been struck and killed by a stone, and—as was often the case with resistance to authority in Scotland—the women of the parish were in the heart of the fight. The authorities who had pulled down the church started to carry off anything of use that they could find. The people of Hassendean chased them down the road, and "engaged them in a sharp conflict" at a place called Hornshole, which is halfway to Hawick. The good people of Hassendean managed to rescue the church-bell from the authorities, and flung it into a deep pool of the river Teviot.

The authorities were so bruised in the encounter that the county sheriff was called out to restore order. It was said that an old woman of Hassendean denounced the sheriff for abetting in the destruction of the church, and foretold the extinction of his lineage by a failure of male heirs.

The parishioners, despite the loss of their church and the threats of the authorities, continued to use the church cemetery for their services, until it was swept away in 1796, when the river Teviot burst its banks.

All is peace and quiet now, the anxieties and conflicts of those days long past. No longer is there even a train's whistle to break the silence, although there is talk of re-building the line, as the population of this border country rises once again after more than a hundred years of decline.

Sollas

Seamus the bus driver says through the window, "I'm going over to Sollas now. If you jump in I'll take you over there and we'll find you a Bed and Breakfast."

He opens the door and I climb in. There's no one else on the bus. It's good to sit down; I'm tired, I've been walking for an hour across a wide, heather strewn landscape.

"Are you here for long?" he asks, half turning in his seat, piloting the bus down the narrow road with one hand. He's got an accent, soft like rain falling on dry grass, different from the locals.

The sky climbs massively overhead, fat with towering cumulus. The air hangs thick and damp. In a month it will be full of midges and horseflies, except when the wind blows. The road cuts across peat hags, threads past lochans and seaweed-fringed inlets from the sea, makes its slow way across the island to the coast. This is North Uist in Scotland's Outer Hebrides, on the rim of western Europe.

"Just a few days. You know, to look around. I've not been out here before." Then, "you're not from here."

"No . . ." he pauses. "Belfast."

"How long have you been up here?"

"Twelve years. It's a good place; you can be alive here." He doesn't say any more about this.

We're driving along beside the water; green shore-grass, brown seaweed; the turquoise sea and flour-white sand laid out like colours on a palette, each one pure and primary, filling the mind like a single thought.

We pass through a ragged village, an irregular line of houses. It's like many old island townships; dismembered during the Clearances, then laid out again by planners to fit the idea of the crofts; each house set to tend its own land.

"It's called Grenitote," says Seamus. "It was all cleared out along here, oh, a hundred and fifty years ago now, in 1849. Then, a while later some of the people were allowed back. There'll be a big celebration this summer for that; to mark the centenary of the time they came back to Sollas. There's been committees working on it."

The houses stand separate from one another, straggling in fits and starts down the line of the road, anti-social and without a core like English villages have. It is barely a community any more.

"I've read about it," I tell him. "Most of the people who lived here were shipped off to Australia."

"The different villages can't seem to get together on it though," he goes on, as if I haven't spoken. "They're all doing separate things for the centenary."

In the morning, I get up early and walk out among the bleating of lambs, down a track towards the sea. The *machair* stretches out thin-green, like cheap baize with the welt showing through. But it holds in its sandy fragility the magic of wild primrose and yellow buttercups, and the nests of skylarks, from which the little birds rise fluttering from level to level, singing all the time until they hover high above everything, as they have always done, even in the sad times.

The islanders gathered seaweed after the winter storms and dug it into the machair: the thin grassland which lies by the sea. The machair is heavy with lime and sand. It must be nourished if it is to produce crops, or feed for the livestock.

Behind the *machair* the beach spreads in a wide curve, deserted but for the calling of gulls and the wash of waves. Once people lived here, walked on these sands and launched boats, and fished these waters. Across the sound to the north, the hills of Harris climb out of the sea.

Late in the summer of 1849 the factor's men came and dragged people out of their homes, and set fire to the dry turf roofs and marram grass thatches. They fired the roofs while there were still people inside the crofts, and furniture and possessions. They burned the houses even when there was tweed on the loom. The tweed, the thick Harris Tweed, was one of the only ways the people could make any income.

The factor's men had been here before this too—a generation earlier—when they sent many Sollas people packing, to Canada. That Clearance was strong in memory still, and so this time the men ran and hid in the windswept hills above the village.

85

I walk along the strand, marvelling at its clean silver softness. The sea slaps against a low, green island to the west of me. A cluster of ruined cottages stands back from the shore, and behind them something larger—burned stone standing gaunt against the sky. This is Vallay, where the Reverend Finlay Macrae, the minister at the time of the 1849 clearance, used to live. You can walk there across damp sand when the tide is out.

The men ran off, but the women stayed by their homes and fought the factor's men with a tenacious passion. The women fought with stones, and wielded the hard tangle-stems of dried kelp like clubs, and drove the attackers off, for a while. But the factor's men came back with the power of the law, and in the end the women were left lying on this beach, bleeding from the battering of police truncheons.

The Reverend Macrae was not only a minister; he was a tenant farmer as well and he dined often at the factor's table. Macrae had three farms—the one on Vallay, and two others over the hill at Baleloch and Griminish on the west coast of the island. He counselled the people of Sollas from his pulpit, telling them to obey the factor and leave. It is God's will, he told them, that they should leave the island and cross the sea. Some of the women attributed the meekness of their menfolk to Macrae's duplicity; his insertion of divine will into a purely secular equation.

The fight between the women of Sollas, and the police and factor's men lasted for several days. It is known in the district as Blar Sholais, the Battle of Sollas. That stream down there is where the women cleaned their wounds, washed the blood from their clothes. It's called Abhainn na Fala, the River of Blood. After the battle most of the women were shipped off to other lands.

I'm standing on the crest of the ridge, near where the men must have hidden in 1849. The plaintive cries of moor birds have followed me up the track, and black and white lap-wings swoop around my head when I pass too close to their nests. The land up here is sparse—coarse hill grass, heather and bare rock swept by salty winds that gather velocity from three thousand miles of Atlantic Ocean. There is no shelter here.

The sea stretches as flat as a plate until it falls over the curve of the earth. A strange, faint pyramid shape lies low down on the horizon as far off as I can see. It floats there, half-in and half-out of the water. It must be St. Kilda, an island so remote I had no idea that it could be seen from here. St. Kilda, abandoned by its inhabitants in the 1930's, forgotten and invisible except on the clearest of days.

In the mid 1800's, the law said that MacDonald of Sleat had ownership of all this land. But the people saw him as the custodian of their rights, the protector of their honour and their livelihoods, and in return for that they had given his house service and loyalty for centuries. They could not believe that he would evict them to make room for sheep. It took a long time for the truth of it to bring out bitter words from one of the local bards.

"Look around you and see the Gentry
With no pity for the poor creatures
With no kindness to their kin . . ."

⌘

The cries of birds fade as I descend to the low ground from this place where the men hid, and the wind is white with the sound of sheep.

Walking the Land of the Picts

The Inverness Traction Company bus carries me down the road beside the Cromarty Firth to Alness. Another bus company moves me on to Tain. Tain is a busy place, an old centre of local government, and a legal seat for this part of the Highlands. On this warm afternoon a traffic warden prowls the High Street, and two policemen investigate a minor traffic accident.

It will be an hour before the Portmahomack bus comes, so I wander into a small, linoleum-floored café for chips and tea. I take a seat at a formica-topped table by the window. Soon my attention is taken up by an incident in the street, a small, strange encounter between a woman and a man.

The woman is in her mid-thirties, poorly dressed in a dark, stained jacket and slacks, her hair dyed blond. An untidy man in a padded jacket and over-long trousers spots

her as she walks down the High Street, and crosses to inter-
cept her. The woman quickens her pace, but the man catches
up to her, then slows down, and follows a step behind. The
man's mouth is moving, although I can't hear what he's saying. A look of pain crosses the woman's face, and she darts
into a shop doorway to get away, but the door is locked. She
crosses the street, and reverses direction back up towards the
chip shop. She holds her hands anxiously out to the people
waiting at the bus stop, but they all turn away. The man
stops, fifteen yards away, and leans against a low wall.

The woman runs back across the High Street to join
two little girls, and walks down the street chattering to them
as if nothing has happened. The man watches her from his
position by the wall, and says something to a scruffy-looking
acquaintance, who has joined him. The woman carries on an
animated conversation with the children. She doesn't look
back. The man shouts something at her from his side of the
street. The children falter and stop, and look back nervously,
but the woman doesn't turn her head. She hurries on, calling the children, and the three of them disappear round the
corner, and exit from the High Street stage. The man pulls a
rolled-up newspaper from his pocket, and continues talking
to his acquaintance as if nothing has happened.

The Portmahomack bus comes and takes me off down
back roads towards Fearn. A wasp buzzes against the windows inside the bus, and causes consternation until a red-
cheeked lady dispatches it with a rolled-up newspaper. The
other passengers give her a brief round of applause.

Fearn stands on a rise above an abandoned airfield, a
village of no more than a few straggling houses, a church and
a tiny railway halt. But its war memorial is packed closely

with names, commemorating sacrifices made when the place must have been much more populous.

Down on the airfield, a tattered windsock hangs from the old control tower, moving gently in the breeze that dries the wheat growing beside the crumbling runways. As far back as the thirteenth century this farmland was known as the most fertile in Scotland.

Lightning struck the old Abbey Church at Fearn during a violent storm one October Sunday in 1742. "The roof of flagstones, with part of a side wall, was beat down in an instant by thunder and lightning," wrote the Bishop Forbes of Ross and Caithness afterwards. It's not clear how many in the congregation were killed in the tragedy, but some suggested the death toll was as high as forty. "The gentry, having luckily their seats in the niches," concluded the bishop, "were saved from the sudden crash, as was the preacher by the sounding boards falling upon the pulpit and his bowing down under it."

The bus drives slowly down the hill to Balintore, and the late afternoon sun lights up the far-away sands on the other side of the Moray Firth at Findhorn. At Hilton of Cadboll, the driver brings the bus to a stop beside the sea, and waits for an old, blind passenger to gather his bearings and his shopping bag and leave the bus. This takes several minutes, but the driver shows great patience. He allows the old man his dignity, doesn't ask him to hurry.

The bus jolts up the peninsula, past small farms and an interesting ruined croft built into an earth bank in the lee of the north wind. Eventually we come to Portmahomack, a village of white houses with neat, painted trim on the coast of a broad firth, facing northwest over the water to the links at Dornoch, and the town of Golspie.

An old church stands on top of a hill behind the village. Students from York University are carrying out an archaeological dig here; already they have uncovered ancient Pictish remains.

The Romans called the people they found in Scotland the Picti, the painted ones. The Picts were fierce fighters, and the disciplined, modern Roman armies were never able to subdue them, although they did win a limited military victory at a place called Mons Graupius. No one knows now where this battle was fought, although some believe it was as far north as the shores of the Moray Firth.

The Picts did some trading with the Romans, but they remained unhappy about the foreign invaders, and periodically fought nuisance campaigns against them. These escalated until the harried northern Roman garrisons called for reinforcements from the south, some thirty years after Mons Graupius.

The 9th Roman Legion—the Hispana, a renowned and ruthless battlegroup with many years of victorious experience in continental wars—marched north from England to sort out the restless Picts once and for all. According to legend, the 9th Legion was never seen or heard from again, its disappearance an enduring mystery.

Soon after this, the Romans, shaken by the loss of the Hispana Legion, and unwilling to continue battling the troublesome Picts, abandoned thoughts of conquering Scotland and drew a military line at Hadrian's Wall, just south of the present day border between Scotland and England.

At first light, a dappled sun illuminates the Duke of Sutherland's monument on top of far-off Ben Bhraggie, and spreads gently over the land. Thin clouds hover over the Ross-shire hills, suggesting a change in the weather. Beneath the window of the room I've taken at the small hotel, a fisherman lays down a net from a small open boat.

After breakfast, I set off up the shore road, past the last two houses of the village, and through a gate onto a thin track. I can follow the coastline north from here, skirting gorse and rocks, tramping over coarse grass to Tarbat Ness, nearly three miles away. There is no clear path here, only sheep tracks. This is rough grazing, outside fenced fields, used only by a few sheep, and sometimes by cattle.

The shore is lined with broken stones and striated sandstone rock. Except for an occasional farmhouse a few fields inland, and some scattered sheep, there is little sign of habitation along the way. An old stone hut with a corrugated tin roof, with boards nailed over its windows and door, stands alone by the sea. A makeshift television aerial, made of coat hangers and wire, hangs from a corner of the roof. The place looks run down and deserted, but the grand vista of sea and sky that stretches in front of it is spectacular, and it would be a fine spot to stay if it keeps dry inside. The cottage sits right at the water's edge, with a view as far as the Sutherland hills. Eighteen rusting spade anchors lie on the grass in front of it, like an enormous, discombobulated plough.

The lighthouse at Tarbat was built by Robert Louis Stevenson's grandfather in the 1830's. It stands distinctively at the point, with two broad red bands about its middle. This promontory was reputedly the site of a Roman fort and, during the Middle Ages, a meeting place for witches and covens. In order to reach the lighthouse I have to cut along the side of one field, and strike diagonally across another, to a high stone wall. The wall encloses the lighthouse and the light-keeper's cottage, and a wasted field bursting with prickly gorse. Cows have been pastured here, and the air is thick with midges and horseflies. The wall runs along to a narrow road, which takes me across a short neck of land to an old pier on the eastern shore. Here, a wooden gate opens onto an ancient path that meanders down the narrow haugh between the cliffs and the shore on the outside coast. This path dates from far-off times, when most travellers would follow the coastline from one place to another rather than try to strike across trackless countryside.

Swallows dive through the hazy summer air, and busy wavelets lap at the rocks. An old rusted winch lies beside the track. Sheep graze the shore grasses, and amble aside as I come up to them. Little else stirs, beyond the seabirds. It's a calm day with a warm sun and a soft breeze, but it's easy to see that this will be a wild coast in bad weather, and the old path difficult to follow around outcrops and cliffs at high tide, or in a storm.

This stretch of coast has ornithological and geographical significance, according to a local information pamphlet. The sea birds can be a nuisance during the breeding season when they sometimes attack visitors. Tarbat Ness is a stopping off point for migratory shearwaters and arctic skuas in autumn—relatives no doubt of the west coast's bonxies. Scandinavian shorebirds frequent the area as well—redwing, meadow pipit and wheatear. Red sandstone forms the main geological formations along this coast, with Jurassic outliers along the shore. The pamphlet mentions oyster plants, although I wouldn't recognise these if I saw them.

There's no sign of anyone else on the track, until I come down the path to Rockfield in the middle of the afternoon. A man and woman are walking on the beach below Ballone Castle. I can tell from their accents that they come from Aberdeen. The lady tells me that they have also hiked down from Tarbat. "It's a shame that no one else is out enjoying such a lovely stretch of coast on such a beautiful day," she says. But I don't mind.

Someone with money is fixing up Ballone Castle. The castle looks more like an ancient keep than a fortification. It's being transformed into a modern country house, and it's far more impressive than its description in my little book of walks, where it's dismissed as a ruin. Now it sits imposingly on top of the cliff, freshly whitewashed, with newly carpentered window frames, and a strong southeasterly view across the sea to the Moray coast.

Rockfield is no more than a row of seashore cottages, and a tiny harbour. Perhaps it was once a fishing village, although it doesn't look old. It might have been built to provide employment for people who were cleared out of the glens in the nineteenth century. The book of walks barely mentions it. It looks more like a neat village of holiday homes than a practical, working community. Several cottage owners have spread their gardens across the right-of-way. The track leads me across someone's driveway, past a front door, squeezes me around parked Range Rovers.

The shore path south of the village is called Rockfield Braes. It's a wide, green haugh, bounded by steep grassy banks, dotted white with grazing sheep. It's easier underfoot here than the track from Tarbat, but it's a long hike from

Rockfield down to Hilton of Cadboll—a good six or seven miles—and it's a warm afternoon.

Long after they'd dispensed with the Romans, the Picts defeated the Angles Germans at Nechtansmere in Angus. The Angles Germans were formidable; they were the descendants of the tribes that had brought down Rome. Later still, the Picts drove off the invading Vikings. They were not to be trifled with, these early Scots, having seen off over a period of centuries the most modern and efficient armies in Europe.

It's believed that the Picts were a matrilineal society; that their bloodlines passed down from their women. Isadore of Seville wrote in the 7th century that the Picts tattooed themselves elaborately, that ". . . their bodies bear designs pricked into their skins by needles".

The Picts left messages to the future, the past and the hereafter on huge tablets, and fragments, of carved stone. The carvings are remarkable, and formalised; some like chain mail, some of them intricately linked, like modern computer designs. Others are more artistically free form, and show exotic, as well as domestic, scenes—like lions disputing a deer's carcass, a running boar, a cow licking clean her calf; or combinations of forms, like a dragon lying amongst spirals.

A burned out cottage stands by itself a few miles down the track. Only the chimney is still standing, gaunt and unsteady. The chimney was made with rough stones, with brick for the firebox, so it's probably not very old—early twentieth century, or late in the nineteenth. The track winds uncertainly past a stack of rocks, and reveals a large cave—the sort of place that wolves might have lived in a thousand years ago.

The sun is high in the sky, and my feet are aching and hot. I take off my shoes and socks and tiptoe into the clear, cold sea. In a few minutes I can feel the salt water putting life back into my feet.

The path opens up again to a wide haugh with tall, ripe grasses waving in the breeze. Mrs. McMahon, who runs the bed and breakfast at Hilton, where I'll stay tonight, told me on the phone not to come before five o'clock, so I lie down by the shore for a nap. A warm wind soothes through the long grass above my head. There are no sheep down here, no animals or people; nothing except for a pair of shags drying their wings on an offshore rock, some gulls overhead, and this long stretch of wild, uninhabited coast.

No Pictish dreams drift through my nap, nor do any particularly Pictish thoughts enter my head along the way. A mile or two before Hilton I come upon an old cottage standing alone above the beach, facing out to sea. Someone is fixing it up, in one of these slow re-building projects that can take years to finish. There's no evidence of any recent work—just torn polythene across the window openings, crackling in the wind. A few yards past the cottage a sign states: *No motor vehicles are to be taken onto Geanies Estate without prior permission.*

The sign faces away from the direction I'm going, and indicates that I'm now leaving Geanies Estate, which I hadn't known I was on. The message makes little sense anyway. It would be difficult to take a vehicle any distance at all along this track. But the sign puts me in mind of Mr. McLeod of Geanies, who was the Sheriff Substitute for this district in the 1790's.

McLeod of Geanies called out the militia from Fort George to put down an insurrection by the people of Strath

Carron and Glen Calvie—glens which are not far from here. McLeod called it an insurrection, but it appears to have been nothing more than a mild, initial protest by people who did not want to be cleared from land that their families had lived on and farmed for generations. But, duly primed, the soldiers marched up from Fort George, and cracked heads, and threw the ringleaders in jail. The courts exiled a number of the miscreants to Australia as an example to the others, and that was the end of it.

This incident was one of the first harsh attacks by the state on the victims of the Highland Clearances, and it was an unsettling precursor of the physical and social violence that was to come. Neither the landowners nor their officers made any provision for the people that they cleared from these glens; made no allowance for the old people, children and women among them; offered no shelter or resettlement. The people who were displaced had no idea what to do, or where to go. In the end they were forced to eke out a living on barren, unproductive land along the rocky coast—land that the landowners had no use for.

Rough shore land, much like I'm crossing now. But wherever McLeod of Geanies wanted the people of Glen Calvie and Strath Carron to go, it was not to his stretch of coastline. Beyond the two derelict habitations I've seen down this long coast there are no other ruins, no sign that anyone has ever worked this ground.

Across a field lies a small fenced area of mounds and depressions, the site of an ancient chapel, and beyond, the first few houses straggle out from Hilton of Cadboll. Back Street leads me down to Sunnyside cottage. Mrs. McMahon is sitting in her front garden with her husband. She takes me upstairs to a bright room, which looks over the rooftops of the houses on Shore street—the only other street in Hilton—and across a wide seascape to the Moray coast in the hazy distance. She brings me a cup of tea, and invites me to come down and sit in her garden.

The tiny garden is bursting with plants—rosemary, clematis, small rhododendrons, and a big, flowering fuchsia. Sweet-smelling chamomile lies between the paving stones, and releases its scent whenever it is crushed underfoot. Mr. McMahon is a long distance bus driver, he tells me. He takes the National Express coach from Inverness to London and back again three times a week. He gets two days off, after this hard, tiring work driving up and down the A9 and the M6.

Sunnyside Cottage is up for sale because the McMahons want to move to Orkney, to live in a croft. Mr. McMahon tells me that he's been offered a driving job up there. If it all works out he will never again have to drive more than fifty miles at a time, because the island where they will live is only twenty-five miles long. He's too old now, he says, to be driving up and down Britain's motorways.

Mrs. McMahon cooks me a tasty pork chop for supper, and confides that the two of them have only been married for a few months. After supper a big pink moon climbs out of the sea. From my room I can see the lights of little towns along the Moray coast—Lossiemouth, Burghead, Findhorn, and Forres, where I was born. It's a full moon and it throws a wide path on the water.

The sun wakes me in the morning, rising quickly out of the North Sea into a deep, red sky. *Red sky at night; shepherd's delight. Red sky in the morning, shepherd's warning . . .*

I'm not hungry but I take a big breakfast anyway. I have a long way to walk today. Mrs. McMahon has placed a cake of blood pudding on the plate with the bacon and eggs. Blood puddin'—beef blood mixed with oatmeal. I don't like it at all. I wonder why they eat it here? Cuisine like this must go back a long way, to a time when people wasted very little, when they used every part of an animal for sustenance. Or perhaps it comes from old ideas about healthy food and culinary delicacies—like salt herring, or kippers, or salted porridge.

Mr. McMahon has long gone to collect his bus and his passengers. His wife tells me that he left for Inverness before seven o'clock. She says he'll be back tomorrow evening, having driven the length of Scotland and England, and back again.

I'm off down the road by ten o'clock. It's a sunny, warm morning, although the wind is starting to rise. The shore road is deserted. It's Sunday morning, and no one is about yet in the seaside villages. Once in a while I catch a glimpse through a window of someone sitting in a dim front room in their Sunday best, waiting for a ride to church. The street unwinds beneath my feet, and Hilton becomes Balintore, and turns into Shandwick, the three villages blended seamlessly together.

It was my intention to follow the shore southwards, all the way round to Nigg, but I can see from the Ordnance Survey map that this will be difficult—even treacherous, if the weather deteriorates. The shore is bounded by great cliffs, which reach all the way round to the Heads, at the entrance to the Cromarty Firth. According to the map, the shore path only goes part of the way. If the weather turns bad these cliffs won't allow any escape from a high, storm-tide.

It will be a better idea today to try and find a path along the top of the cliffs, so I turn away from the sea and follow the road up a hill, towards a tall Pictish standing stone. The stone is known as Clach a'Charridh, and the antiquities people have encased it in a great glass box to protect it from the weather. No one knows whether the stone stands in its original position. It was blown down in a storm in 1846 and broken, and later mended. One side of it has a carving of a cross, made up of angels, beasts, and protruding bosses—and inter-twined snakes. The other side of the stone is laced thick with Pictish symbols, interlacing spiral shapes, animals, men and riders.

At the top of the hill, a lady in a red sweater is standing at the door of a cottage, holding a baby and watching two tractors turn a small field of hay. I stop to ask her the way.

"I don't think there is a path round to Nigg by the shore, although I'm not positive," she says. "But if you stay on this road for a mile or two, you'll find a track that will take you up onto the hill." She gives me directions.

The abandoned airfield that I saw from the bus near Fearn reveals itself again from the main road, its tattered windsock still swinging from its derelict control tower. The airfield was built during the First World War to protect the big naval base at Invergordon.

There's hardly any traffic on the road, but I don't stay on it for long. In half a mile I turn off on a track which climbs up beside a field of barley. A herd of cows stands on a wide shoulder of the hill and gazes down at me, blocking the path. The animals move reluctantly aside as I reach them. The track crosses a cattle grid, and goes up a steep gradient on a narrow roadway made of concrete slabs. The slabs were probably laid down during the Second World War, when there were important lookout posts and gunnery emplacements on these hills.

Scattered copses lie across the top of the slope, and the track eases past fields that are split with lines of gorse. There is a fine view up here. I can see dark weather coming in from the southwest, reaching black fingers up the length of the Cromarty Firth, and blanketing the Ross-shire hills behind Evanton, Alness and Invergordon. Another herd of cows straggles across the track. When they catch sight of me they turn to stare, and stop.

One of the beasts is bigger than the rest. As I move closer, it shoulders one of the cows roughly out of its way. It's a bull that the farmer has put out among his cows, and the bull lifts a hoof and thumps it on the ground. He's not at all keen about having someone else in his territory. I retreat as discreetly as I can, until I'm safely under the brow of the hill, and out of his sight. He doesn't follow me, but I can hear his trumpeting and rutting reverberating across the hillside for the next hour.

There's no question of continuing along the track because of the bull, but I don't want to go all the way back down to the road. I spend a few minutes scanning the hillside, and its gullies and woods, but the choice of routes across the broken ground is limited. I set off across a corner of the cow field, and negotiate a gully full of bracken and prickly gorse. This is barely preferable to going back to the road, for I get well scratched-up by bramble thorns in the gully, before I stagger out into a sheep field.

Cheviot sheep turn their heads to stare. Half a dozen Scots pines stand up at the crest of the hill, and the view opens out until I can see the whole coastline that I walked yesterday. The villages I passed through this morning are set neatly along the shore below my feet. Beyond them, the coast edges summer fields all the way back to Tarbat Ness and its pencil-thin lighthouse. Dornoch and Golspie are faint in the distance, against the Sutherland hills.

I'm standing on Kraken Hill, its name an old Pictish name. It feels like a place where people once lived. Two substantial heather-covered knolls stand below me, directly atop the sea-cliffs. They look as if they could have been encampment sites in ancient times. Both knolls offer good views all around—would have offered protection from marauders. Neither of them are conspicuous, because they are not the highest points of land.

Whitecaps froth on the sea below, and the distant Moray coast scuds in and out of dark rain showers. To the west, the black weather is closer now. It lies ominously behind Tain, and has already blotted out the Ross-shire hills. But I'm hot after the climb, and it's still dry up here.

A belt of impenetrable gorse channels me back to the west, high above a deep cleft that I'll have to find some way to cross. A sheep track takes me half a mile inland before I can find a way down to a stream at the foot of the gully. A pair of slippery birch logs lie across the stream, and I balance across them like a circus acrobat. Staccato rain starts to fall, but it only lasts for a minute. I climb through a wood, which changes character as the land rises, and turns into an old, open Scots pine plantation, with a carpet of heather and moss underfoot. A firm track carries me higher, back towards the sea.

The cart track skirts the Hill of Nigg. Nigg, another ancient place name from Pictish times. Many places in this area—with names like Tarbat, Cadboll, Kraken, Sutor—are quite different from the traditional Scots and Scandinavian root-names that I'm used to. Another belt of rain passes across the hill, and forces me to find shelter under a pine tree.

The rain starts to come in waves, with about ten minutes between each squall. The Black Isle vanishes, and Cromarty is blotted out to a blur. I walk on during the breaks between squalls, and shelter from another shower beneath a lone hawthorn at the edge of a muddy field on the exposed southwest side of the hill. My feet are soaked and muddy from walking across waterlogged fields. A bog bars the way, and forces me back up the hill so I can skirt around it. Another shower comes before I'm ready for it, and I dive under some gorse bushes. The wind picks up, and the rain flies in horizontally. My jacket springs leaks. But there is no other shelter up here, so I crouch disconsolately under the gorse for an hour, until the rain stops.

Cows make a mess of the ground at gates, and anywhere else that the land has a tendency to turn to marsh. Another impassable bog forces me to make a complicated manoeuvre along a slippery, rickety fence in order to reach dry ground that has been broken and turned by the plough. It's ground full of thistles and nettles, and I stumble off the tops of big divots, and turn my ankles.

Eventually the path re-establishes itself, and takes me up the last heights above the entrance to the Cromarty Firth, to old Second World War lookouts. The Moray coast is a distant suggestion, just visible through the rain. The going is easier now; another field of sheep, and then I'm in amongst the old military installations at North Sutor. These rusting gunnery stations once guarded the entrance to the naval anchorage at Invergordon, when it was one of the Royal Navy's main wartime bases. Derelict gun emplacements and bunkers sit silent and incongruous in the face of the older history of this land; a history which still animates this place with its spirits.

The rain starts to bucket down again, and drives me into an old wartime barrack that has been turned into a cattle byre. It's a filthy concrete shed, and it stands in murky cloud, high above the entrance to the Firth. But it's either this, or head out into the lashing rain. The downpour lasts for an hour, and when it stops I follow an overgrown track across the shoulder of the hill to watery sunshine, and a view down the length of the Cromarty Firth to Dingwall. The village of Cromarty lies quietly below, on the far side of the narrows. The little ferryboat is halfway across, looking like a toy on the flat water.

This is the King's ferry. It was an important crossing in the Middle Ages, when there were few roads and the Scottish kings found it difficult to control their northern lands. Late in the twelfth century, King William the First established a castle here at Dunskaith to protect the ferry crossing, and granted land to support it, and revenues from the ferry.

The track winds past an enormous pit filled with discarded barbed wire, which lies rusting in masses of coils, like some witless mechanical monster. This path was probably once able to carry motor vehicles, but gorse and brambles have claimed it back and narrowed it, so that it's useful now only to sheep. The path becomes steeper as it descends. It tracks across the face of the hillside above Nigg, and comes eventually to a tarmac road which leads down to the village.

I take a room for the night at the Nigg Ferry Inn. It's five o'clock, but I'm not hungry, although I haven't had any lunch. I'm tired and wet, so I run a hot bath. As soon as I turn on the taps the showerhead sprays wildly round the bathroom, and soaks all the towels.

The inn sits in a prime location by the sea, and might have been quite fine once. But now it's a scruffy little hotel, run by people who don't seem to have any experience in the hospitality business. The carpets are worn, and the walls of the lobby show signs of rising damp. My room is painted puce-pink, and smells of stale cigarette smoke. The window looks onto an abandoned naval yard, strewn with old oil drums and pieces of rusting machinery. A huge, black metal hangar stands in the middle of the yard, missing corrugated sheets from its walls. Pieces of torn polythene are stuck in the fence, and crackle like machine guns in the wind.

When I turn up for breakfast in the morning the English proprietor looks at me in surprise. "I didn't know you were staying at the hotel," he says. "We didn't expect an extra person for breakfast."

I'm not sure what to say. I missed lunch and dinner yesterday, and now I'm starving. "You were speaking to the girl at the front desk last night when I checked in," I tell him. "Surely you noticed me then."

He's nice enough, but my appearance has thrown him—despite the fact that only one small family of four is sitting in the dining room, and there is no sign of any other guests. I can't believe that one extra breakfast can be much of a strain on the inn's resources.

The inn's furniture looks as if it has been picked up in jumble sales in different parts of the country. None of it matches. Odd chairs stand around uneven tables. A framed print of Damon Hill at the wheel of a Formula One racing car fills one wall. The Nigg Ferry Inn has become a place without charm, despite its interesting setting among such history and character. When I leave, the proprietor charges me an excessive £27 for bed and breakfast.

While I'm waiting at the landing for the first ferry to Cromarty, I take a wander down the sandy beach in front of the inn. I can see from here that I would never have been able to get round the Head by following the shore. Tumbled and broken by rock slides, the cliffs fall sheer to the water.

It's low tide and the single car that the ferry brings from Cromarty has to disembark onto the shingle, and then drive up the concrete ramp. I'm the only passenger heading for Cromarty this morning. The deckhand takes £2 for the fare and retreats back into the wheelhouse. He sits down beside the captain, and the two of them spend the crossing reading the morning paper, scarcely glancing out of the window to check that we're heading in the right direction. The Cromarty Rose is the smallest ferryboat in Britain, and this is the last of the many ferry crossings that once spotted the King's road from Inverness to his northern domains.

"Can you tell me if there's a bus to Inverness?" I ask the deckhand, as the ferry nudges the ramp at Cromarty.

"Oh, there'll be a bus schedule pasted on the lamp-post by the football pitch," he says. "Just walk up the main street and turn right at the end. You'll find it there."

The Inverness Traction schedule I have in my bag shows only one bus a week from Cromarty to Inverness, and that's on Wednesdays—two days from now. But the poster stuck to the lamp-post lists an hourly service with a company called Rapsons.

A bus is sitting at the side of the road with its engine idling. I tap on the driver's window and ask him where he's going. Down the firth, past Jemimaville he says, left at the 'T' junction, and over the hill to Rosemarkie and Fortrose, eventually on to Inverness. He tells me he'll make the same trip again in the afternoon.

"I think I'll catch you later in the day then, somewhere down the road." I tell him. "It's too fine a day not to walk for a while." I turn my back on Cromarty and set off down the shore road, casting westwards for Jemimaville and Balblair. This pretty country road is no chore at all, the walking easy after the trackless hills and rutted shore paths of yesterday.

A stiff wind is blowing up the firth from the southwest, but the sky tells me the morning will stay clear and warm. The high cirrus clouds look harmless enough for today, although they could be forecasting a change in the weather for tomorrow. Whitecaps dance around a pair of oilrigs anchored out in the firth. The rigs have been brought in for maintenance, and now they're full of workmen. Loudspeaker announcements, and hammerings and bangings, float over the water to the shore road.

The road is bathed in sunshine and fresh air, and offers expansive vistas of the firth and the Ross-shire hills. Salt-tangle smells rise from the nearby strand, and dilapidated weed-grown racks lie half out of the water—set out years ago to promote the growth of oysters and mussels.

This great firth was once given to the keepers of the castle at Dunskaith, the protectors of the ferry crossing. "I have a certain harbour or bay," boasted Sir Thomas Urquhart of Cromarty in 1653, "in goodness equal to the best in the world. Ten thousand ships together may within it ride, in the greatest tempest that is, as in a calm."

The air turns soft and muggy as the morning wears on. The sky reflects the change. Bad weather is coming up in the southwest. Dark clouds roll over the mountains, part as they wheel up to the base of the Black Isle, and funnel off to the left and right—south of the Beauly Firth to Inverness on one side; to the hills behind Alness and Invergordon on

108

the other. The hills on the north side of the Cromarty Firth already look fuzzy and wet. But here on the Black Isle the wind stays warm, the sky sunny.

An old folks' home sits next to a straggle of cottages near Jemimaville. This cluster of houses doesn't seem to have a name, although when I look later at the map, it's noted as Shoremill; a place I've never heard of before. The people in the cottage gardens look as if they're retired, as if they're waiting to move into the old people's home next door.

Two fields beyond Shoremill a grey hawk sits on a fence post at the side of the road. Or he might be a kite or a buzzard; I don't know the local birds well enough to tell. Half a dozen swallows are dive-bombing him, flying straight and fast, and veering off at the last split-second. The hawk tries to ignore the swallows but they're too aggressive; he flies off in search of peace, and settles in a small tree.

A plaque on a stone cairn offers information on the history of the naval anchorages in the roads. The base at Invergordon was active from the middle of the nineteenth century, to its peak during the First World War, and again in the Second. In its day it was one of the biggest naval anchorages in the world. After the war it was gradually abandoned; given over first to the gulls, and later to the oilrigs.

The photographs on the plaque were taken during the First World War, and it's strange now to see what a crowded, thriving place this once was. It must have been a sight to stand here, with the ships of the Royal Navy spread across the firth, filling it from end to end. There were protective fighter airfields at Nigg and Alness, and seaplane bases scattered around the shores of the firth. These airfields are abandoned now, but they were busy and important in their day. Economic development officials have been eyeing the old

109

airfield at Alness recently, and it is slowly being re-incarnated as an industrial park. The naval wharves and shore installations at this end of the firth are used today by oil industry supply companies as they build, maintain, and re-furbish the big North Sea drilling rigs.

The postman motors past in his red van, doing his rounds in Jemimaville. This short, single-street village has a name that's incongruous to Scotland. It sounds as if it has been borrowed from deepest Alabama. An important consultation is going on as I walk past the garage. A small group stands around a car. A mechanic is bent over, staring at the engine. He straightens up, and scratches his head. The post office is a tiny red-painted shed. It is the only building that sits on the left side of the road. No one in the village acknowledges my passing at all.

I come upon a sign which points to a bird sanctuary. This corner of the firth is home to many different species of water birds. Two wooden sheds stand at the edge of a salt-water marsh. These are hides, built so that passers-by can observe the birds in the tidal wetlands.

A pair of ornate stone gateposts stands at the side of the road, and a gravel driveway curves through a wood to a big country house. A sign at the gate states that this is a herb farm, open from one till five on weekday afternoons. But it's only noon, and I don't have any immediate use for herbs.

A road junction stands between wheat fields. The right turn goes to Balblair and the road up the firth to Culbokie, eventually to the bridge over to Evanton and Dingwall. It's a good fifteen miles to Dingwall, my ultimate destination, but the Rapson's bus driver told me that he doesn't go that way. I don't want to walk another fifteen miles today, so I strike off on a road which snakes up a hill towards Rosemarkie and

Fortrose. These two adjacent villages lie to the south, on the Moray Firth shore of the Black Isle.

It's a long, slow haul over the ridge in the middle of the Black Isle, past fields filled with roundels of wheat and barley. The sun is coming down hard. The cooling wind that met me along the seashore has vanished, sucked in by the thick woods on each side of the road. The road stretches pencil straight for a mile in front of me, no longer as interesting as it was.

Midges and horseflies congregate in fierce clouds wherever there are trees and animals. This part of the Black Isle is given over to market gardens and hobby-farms, more tamed than the north shore. Eventually the road brings me to Rosemarkie, and the temptation to stop at a stylish pub, called the Plough, in the middle of the village. But I resist this; the bus will be along soon.

The centre of Rosemarkie is pretty, with houses built out to the edge of the street in the nineteenth century style of Scottish artisans. Unfortunately the authorities, recognising the value of this place as part of an expanding commuter belt for Inverness, have allowed ugly sub-divisions to sprout at the edges of town. But these observations are interrupted by the bus, which comes to carry me off to Inverness. There I hop on another bus, which takes me to Dingwall.

It has been good to walk with the Picts, who are a largely forgotten people now. It has been good to share in a small, elemental way their landscape, and by doing that, to gain a sense of the kind of people they might have been.

Wick

The best time to be about is early morning, when everyone is still asleep, when the air is cool and fresh. I'm waiting on the platform at Dingwall for the first train to Wick. Dingwall is an old market town to the north of Inverness, busy when the livestock sales are on, but otherwise a sleepy place. It's Saturday, and there's not a cloud in the sky. No one else is about, except for an old lady reading a newspaper. On the way to the station I'd gone to the bank machine to get some money, and found that Friday-night revellers had turned over a big flower barrel in front of the National Hotel.

The train pulls in from Inverness. There are only four passengers on board. The old lady and I climb on. The carriages grind reluctantly out of the station, and over the Peffery River, which slides between rich mud banks. Dingwall falls behind as the train rumbles along by the sea, just above

112

the high tide line. Southwards, across the Cromarty Firth, the Black Isle is ripe with wheat, and morning sunshine. The train turns inland for Tain, and passes by the Hill of Nigg that I traversed last weekend. It looks like a big hill from the train, long and rambling, bigger than it seemed when I walked it.

From Tain, the train passes along the shore of the Dornoch Firth. The water is flat calm, and reflects perfectly the hills and fields on the north side. Ducks scatter, and leave slow-motion tracks across the water's surface as the train rattles past. A heron fishes patiently among reeds. Near Ardgay, at the mouth of Strath Carron, swans drift pure white in front of a light, floating mist.

You can pass the time on trains, conjuring up histories of the other passengers. A middle-aged man in the carriage has a flattened, boxer's face. He's wearing blue jeans, and his sleeves are rolled up above bony elbows. Thin and gaunt, he has a kind of weathered, Australian look about him. From time to time he gives a deep-chested, hacking cough. It seems to me as if he's come up here on his last journey, perhaps to see where his people came from before they were cleared out of the glens and shipped to the Antipodes.

The man gets off the train at Lairg, and greets a woman on the station platform in a voice with a slight North American accent. Then he hoists an enormous pack onto his back—a pack complete with a tent, sleeping bag and carry-mat—and bounds up a steep flight of stairs, two at a time. He looks fit and lean as he trots over the bridge. He drops his pack on the far platform, and starts tossing heavy bundles of morning newspapers into a red van, as if he's done it all before.

At Rogart, in the next glen, the train passes a sign with an arrow. *Memorial cairn to Sir John A. MacDonald, first Prime Minister of Canada.* The glen is pretty and bucolic in the morning sun, with neat, white houses and well-kept fields backed by craggy, heather-covered hills. It looks like the kind of place where two of Sir John's most enduring character traits—an aptitude for procrastination, and an affinity for strong drink—might have originated.

The train glides back to the coast, and passes an old stone Broch at Golspie. Dunrobin Castle stands near here, where the Duke of Sutherland had his estate. Sutherland was the landowner responsible for some of the worst land clearances of the nineteenth century. His statue stands high above the town, on top of round-backed Ben Bhraggie, visible for miles up and down the coast. History doesn't paint Sutherland as the kind of active man who would have been likely to climb up the hill where his statue stands, and local people—with a suitable lack of respect—refer to the statue as "The Mannie". The train passes through the little station that the Duke built for his entourage, for his factors and gillies, and his hunting parties. The station's fret-worked buildings are clean and freshly painted, but the platform is green with moss.

The landscape around Brora is broad and flat, scattered before the hills with crofts, like the settlements on Scotland's west coast. The sea is calm all the way down past the Tarbat peninsula to the Moray coast. Shore birds with long curved beaks scuttle across the sand, and shags stand up on rocks like thunderbirds, with their wings stretched out to dry. Shags are diving, fishing birds, similar to cormorants. But unlike cormorants they don't have waterproof oils in their feathers, and they must dry themselves out every time they

114

get wet, otherwise they can't fly. They do this by standing motionless on rocks, and holding their wings out with the feathers splayed, like carved Greek icons.

At Helmsdale, where the hills fall abruptly into the sea, the train turns inland and starts the long climb up the Strath of Kildonan. This glen is narrow near its mouth, with a thin haugh of fertile land lying by the river. Ruined crofts cling to narrow ledges along the sides of the valley, high above the good bottom land. These crofts are the remains of the tiny smallholdings where the people who had been cleared from Kildonan, Kinbrace, and Altnabreac, and the other settlements further up the strath, tried to eke out a living. This is the glen that John Diefenbaker's mother's family came from—the root soil of another Canadian prime minister. Gold was discovered here in the Helmsdale River during the eighteen-sixties—enough of it to attract prospectors from as far away as the Yukon.

The railway line claws painstakingly up to a far-reaching landscape that stretches to a horizon of distant mountains etched against an enormous, blue sky. On this clear day nothing moves on this unbounded moorland, nothing to indicate that anything at all lives up here. When I last came up here the air was hard with sleet, and I saw great herds of red deer sheltering near the railway line, their backs white with snow.

This uncompromising wilderness presented a harsh natural barrier to transportation and communication right up to the end of the nineteenth century. Until then, most people who journeyed in or out of the north country went by sea, although the coast up here is a wild and dangerous one—so dangerous, that few of the people who lived up here ever travelled any distance at all, and there was little communication with the rest of the country. As a result, the communities up here evolved without much external influence. They developed their own customs, habits and traditions, separate from the rest of Scotland, different from societies in the south. Even today there are few roads up here, and this landscape—known as the 'flow' country—remains virtually uninhabited, the railway its main lifeline.

At the watershed, the train releases energy like a spring, and races off down the brae towards the fertile valley which lies between Thurso and Wick—past standing stones, and rounded hills permeated with burial chambers. The guard walks down the carriage to say that all passengers for Wick have to change to another train at Georgemas Junction, near Halkirk, as this train is going straight on to Thurso.

A man with a limp and a woman with a shopping bag are the only other passengers on the two-carriage train to Wick. The train sets off across bleak brush land, and enters a green, shallow vale. This is the Watten Valley, a contrast to the bleak moors we crossed a short time ago.

The soil in the Watten Valley has been fed for centuries by rich sea tangle hauled up from the seashore by cottars—smallhold crofters. The lush yields of barley that were produced across this fertile northland were enough by the end of the eighteenth century to support nearly a hundred distilleries in the county of Caithness. In 1793, the Reverend William Smith, minister of the parish of Bower, complained that the " . . . number of small distilleries are very unfavourable both to the health and morals of the [tenant farmers], especially on account of the consumption in public meetings or at markets and country fairs."

A stream flows down the centre of the valley to a loch, where fishermen are casting for trout. They sit patiently in green clinker boats, these fishermen, watching their floats bob on the water, much as their fathers and grandfathers did before them. Loch Watten appears many times in references to my family, as they farm, and travel back and forth down the years across this landscape.

Fields of bright yellow barley slope gently up from the loch. Much of the crop has already been brought in. On farms where it has still to be harvested there's an urgency to get the reaping finished before the weather breaks. Farmers are working all across the countryside over the weekend, harvesting from early in the day until dark. The massive Claes combine harvesters block the narrow by-ways as they shuttle from one farm to another, stretching over the centre line on the country roads, causing hold-ups in the local traffic. These big machines are far too expensive for the farmers to own, and so they're rented from contractors for the harvest.

Each generation of my family produced a multitude of children; at least five or six, often as many as nine and ten. My grandmother had five brothers and sisters, and a regiment of cousins. It's strange to think of all those lives, and wonder what happened to them—all those people down the centuries; names now on gravestones in local churchyards.

Ceenie lived near here, an elderly aunt now gone, a cousin of my grandmother's. Ceenie had to walk every day to school in Keiss—two and a half miles each way. She would stop at Mr. Henderson the blacksmith's on her way home, for creamy milk and bere scones.

Ceenie and her brothers and sisters had a little blue and white donkey cart. One day, when cousin Donald came down from his parents' farm at Holland Mey, he decided to unhitch the donkey and pull the cart himself. So he set the donkey free, the children all jumped in, and Donald took up the slack.

"Down the avenue we all went in great style, with Donald running very fast," said Ceenie. "Suddenly the cart toppled over and we all went into the ditch. The cart was bent and broken, and the donkey wandered off. There was trouble about that; my mother was always glad to see Donald, but she was always relieved to see him go home again."

Donald went on to win a Military Cross in the First World War, and shocked the family by marrying a London chorus girl.

My grandmother's cousin Henry lived near here too, at the turn of the twentieth century. Henry walked nearly three miles every day to school, in all weathers, summer and winter. He wore the kilt to school, but he couldn't stand to wear the cocked bonnet that went with it. On his way out of the house he'd take an old cap of his father's off the peg at the front door, and hide it under his coat. When he was out of sight of the house he'd take off his bonnet and tuck it behind a drystane dyke, and wear his father's cap the rest of the way to school.

I don't know any of the family who live up here now, so when the train pulls in to Wick I start telephoning around to find lodgings. The landlady at the Quayside Inn tells me that she has a room, and gives me directions. Her little bed & breakfast sits right on Wick's fishing harbour, and the room is a fair price. I dump my bag, and go out right away for a walk, to shake off the cobwebs from the train journey.

The way to the coast path takes me up to the streets and tenements and grey stone houses of an old part of Wick called Pultneytown. I don't know the derivation of this name,

118

but some of my grandmother's family came down the valley to live here in the early eighteen hundreds.

Curtains blow out of open windows in the breeze, and children dash in and out of alleyways. A marmalade cat runs across the road and dives under a parked car. The harbour falls away behind, empty but for a brace of fishing boats moored at the wharf.

My great-great-great-grandfather's brother, James Finlayson, came down the Watten Valley from the family's farm to live here in 1810, soon after his seventeenth birthday. The farm at Aucorn was too small to accommodate seven grown-up children, and the tenancy passed on to one of James's older brothers. So, instead of following in the family tradition of farming, James came to Pultneytown and apprenticed as a cooper, a skilled barrel maker. Coopers were much in demand towards the end of the Napoleonic Wars, mainly for making the 'slack' barrels required for transporting processed fish, but also to make the 'tight' casks which could hold whisky.

Once I bought a bottle of Scotch for a friend who wanted to try a whisky that he couldn't buy in Canada. The whisky I bought him was called Old Pulteney. It had a gentle taste, sweet with soft peat from the moors, and accents from the sea, and a hint of the north wind. It was made here in Wick, and it came from the distillery where James had once made barrels. My friend says it was the best whisky he's ever had.

James's son Donald also went into the cooperage, and by the time he was twenty-three, in 1850, he had completed his apprenticeship. Donald Finlayson married Elizabeth McKenzie in the Pultneytown Free Presbyterian Church

119

on June 7th of that year. Fourteen days after the wedding, Donald sailed with his new bride from Scrabster Roads near Thurso, on the Stettin barque *Argo*, bound for Canada.

"We sailed . . . with wind ahead. Most of the passengers got seasick that night," wrote Donald in his diary, after that first day at sea.

The coast path follows the shoreline, past great slab rocks set above the sea like flagstones. The rock is perfect for quarrying as it splits along well-defined seams. It has been the main building material up here for centuries. It is evident in the walls of houses and barns, and farm fences are made from these slabs, standing up on end like close-packed tombstones.

The path goes down a lane to a stone wall and a stile, and leads across a field to a ruined castle, which stands on the lip of a cliff. This is Wick Castle, built in the twelfth century by Harald Maddadson, an Earl of Caithness. There isn't much left of the castle now, although a pair of walls remain standing to a height of two or three storeys. The ruin sits on a slender finger of rock and grass that juts out to sea with sheer drops on either side. It can only be reached by crossing a narrow isthmus that was originally protected by a deep ditch and a drawbridge.

The property is maintained by Historic Scotland, who have built a sturdy wooden gate into the fence. The gate is strong and simple in design and makes me think of Em's father, an old Newfoundland carpenter who would approve of its functional artistry.

The land is flat on top of the cliffs and fenced for grazing; the fields are populated with sheep and cattle, and at one place, Jacob goats. The path is narrow, and inches away from deep, sheer drops to sharp rocks and the sea. Terns and arctic skuas and the occasional gull patrol the cliff edges, and eye strangers attentively. I lie down in the long grass and study these birds. They fly well in the uncertain air currents at the cliff-top, making tiny adjustments to the angle of their wings, flexing their tip feathers, using their heads to adjust the airflow, their feet as rudders. I can hear skylarks. Buttercups lie underfoot, and delicate harebells and ling heather, and long, wild grasses. The air today is clear for miles out to sea.

It was different than this when Donald and Elizabeth made their Atlantic crossing, even though it was midsummer. Much of Donald's diary is taken up with comments about weather, which was a matter of importance to everyone on board the sailing ship.

Friday July 5th, 1850
The wind a little fair in the morning, but against us in the afternoon, blowing strong towards night but veered round very suddenly and blew a complete hurricane, which none on board ever witnessed before. The masts expected to fall overboard every minute for the space of three hours and not a stitch of canvas up, so that we were obliged to run under bare poles until the wind abated very little, when they were able to get up two trisails and hove her to. Passengers altogether at their wits end with the ship rolling so heavy that it turned the boxes and chests from one side to another; hatches closed.

Donald fished one day during the voyage to Canada, on the banks of Newfoundland. It was a rare chance to vary a dull shipboard diet with something fresh. Even then, a hundred and fifty years ago, the Grand Bank was a crowded place, and because there were so many vessels, it was dangerous in fog.

Wednesday, July 24th, 1850

Becalmed. Tried the cod fishing and succeeded. The women of the second cabin, four in number, got a fine dinner from the Captain in his own cabin. The wind sprung up towards night. Passed an iceberg in sight of Newfoundland.

Two small fishing boats pass close inshore, checking lobster pots and looking for crab. Half a mile out a pair of bigger boats make wide sweeps as they cast their nets. Far, far down the coast, two oilrigs nestle in the crook of the Moray and Ross-shire coastlines, some ten miles offshore.

I pick my way down to the end of the path, and follow a fence for a while, skirting cliffs above wild indentations and fantastic geologies, and staring down on seabird colonies. This coastline is like a place of pirates and smugglers, riddled with secret sea caves, with deep green seawater reflecting sunlight seductively into hidden grottos.

A narrow meadow is draped along the top of the cliffs, and scattered with lichen-stained, granite rocks. To reach it I have to traverse a stone dyke. I've almost reached the dyke on a small rabbit trail when a fox starts up right at my feet, and lopes off towards the sea. He gives me a fright, hidden as he was in the lee of the wall, so close and so perfectly blended into his landscape; but he's a fine, shifty-looking creature, and his big incongruous tail floats along behind him like red dust as he makes off. He keeps glancing back at me, a lovely rust colour now against the green hillside, slowing as he turns to ascertain my intentions. He trots around the end of a drystane wall, and makes his way across a sloping pasture. He stops on the skyline for a minute to stare back, and then he's gone.

A large bird flies out from the cliffs and begins climbing the air currents. The bird is grey underneath, and as it banks I can see its top feathers are golden-brown. It doesn't look big enough to be an eagle, although it might be a young one. A moment later a fast-flying bird with angled, corsair's wings skims over my head. I think it's a falcon, and wish I knew more about them so I could be sure.

I've walked more than four miles now, and it's time to turn round and head back to Wick. A herd of cows takes great interest in me on the way back. I can tell from the way they stop eating and lift their heads to stare, that my passing is probably the most interesting event of their day. A bull stands alone in another field, but there are two fences between us, so I don't pay him any attention. Pultneytown's grey slate roofs shine dull across the afternoon fields in the waning sun, and gradually Wick reveals itself, cuddled in the hollow where the river flows into the sea.

When they reached Canada, Donald and Elizabeth lived at first in Dundas, Ontario, not far from the busy, industrial centre of Hamilton. It was a big contrast to the rural, fisheries-based environment of Wick. Two years later they moved to Paris, Ontario, and Donald found work as a cooper again, making the barrels that were used to store powdered Plaster of Paris, which was becoming valuable in immobilising, and healing, broken limbs.

Donald prospered, and in less than four years the rest of his family—including his parents—joined him in Canada. In the course of time Donald and Elizabeth had nine children, all of them born in Canada. In 1873, James, one of Donald's boys, became a Trooper in the first intake of Sir John A. MacDonald's brand new North West Mounted Police.

In the morning, the Citylink bus takes me away from Wick. The road skirts the wild interior moors, keeping close to the well-farmed coastal strip. It's another warm day with broken cloud, and the bus follows the road south through tiny villages with Nordic, northern names—Thrumster, Ulbster, Lybster.

Generations of young women from my family came to work in these towns and villages. Some of the girls came to serve in the manses at Latheron and Latheronwheel, sometimes to teach the minister's children. The family believed that an appointment at the manse would give the girls prospects for a good marriage; that influential people from the surrounding countryside—farmers and physicians and teachers—would call upon the minister, and thus give the girls valuable social exposure.

They have strong names, these places, but I'm not sure what it is they evoke, and I am ignorant of most of their derivations. Latheron is the sort of name we can almost understand; it has an Anglo-Saxon ring to it. The village is small and scattered, and sits just below the south-facing crest of a hill, looking over a deep glen.

Latheronwheel lies lower down the same glen, with a harbour which fits neatly into the tiny, narrow mouth of the valley. The origin of this place-name seems obscure too, unless 'wheel' means something diminutive or descriptive in one of the old Nordic languages. Each of the villages has two or three churches, which seems a great number in relation to their size.

The bus climbs another hill, and makes its way down the steep, southern side towards Dunbeath. The driver engages bottom gear, and gingerly negotiates a series of hairpin bends, before coming safely to the bottom. Like most of the villages on this stretch of coast, Dunbeath lies at the foot of a deep glen beside a river, near the sea. A sign at the entrance to the village states *Birthplace of the writer Neil Gunn*. The bus starts up the opposite hillside. Dunbeath is a pretty place on such a sunny day, but it will be bleak in winter. The sun will not shine very often here when the days are short.

This road is shorter than the rail journey, which makes its circuit through the interior of Caithness. We're soon past Helmsdale and Brora and Golspie, jolting towards the south. Then we're across the Dornoch Firth, and racing past Tain, heading for Invergordon and Alness, and on down the Cromarty Firth—until I have an urge to leave the bus at the south end of the Cromarty Bridge.

The Black Isle

The bus drops me at the road end on the south side of the Cromarty Bridge. The wind is flying as I step across the main Inverness road and duck down a lane between wheat fields. The sound of traffic recedes; white horses chase each other across the Cromarty Firth to its north shore and Dingwall, which rambles up a hillside below threatening clouds. But I know the Black Isle will keep me from the weather; these dark, westerly clouds part when they reach here, and scatter off to north and south.

The lane meanders past graveyards, and churches that are old and unkempt, from another time. Far more people lie in these graveyards than live here now. At tiny Urquhart, two churches and two full graveyards stand amidst a collection of houses, speaking to a time before this land was cleared of people; a time when it supported a much larger

126

population than it does now. A neat sign by the graveyard gate states "No dogs allowed". Oaks and Italian cypress trees border the lane.

The northern kirk didn't like anyone to do any work on Sundays. Ceenie's mother often had the minister over for supper, but the dishes couldn't be washed until Monday morning—a long time to leave things for a family of eight, after three or four Sunday visitors. There was no stainless steel then, so the knives were cleaned with bath brick, a kind of pumice stone. One Sunday night, Ceenie's sister Jane couldn't stand the mess, and quietly washed up, disguising her sin by placing a dirty plate on top of the pile of clean dishes.

A sad, bramble-wracked ruin stands by itself in the middle of a barley field, on a seaward-facing slope. Empty windows stare north like sightless eyes at the square, table-shape of Ben Wyvis. Blackberries border the lane in ripe profusion. The afternoon has made me thirsty and I eat the blackberries greedily, heavy as they are on the vine, and sweet with juice. There are so many of them that I am profligate, discarding any with the slightest blemish.

A farmer harvests his wheat, cutting into the tall stalks with a big combine harvester. He must bring his crop in before the weather turns. These heavy clouds will not contrive to miss the Black Isle for much longer. It is already September, and soon there will be rain and cold winds.

The light changes across the water, and settles like a corona over the fields behind the hill known as the Cat's Back, etching against it the dark stonework of Hector MacDonald's tower on the crest above Dingwall. Sunlight illuminates a ribbon of road which winds round the hill from Brahan, the home of the famous seer. Beyond that, the clouds lift from the face of Ben Wyvis, and reveal its broad, round back.

The Brahan Seer had the gift of 'the sight'. Hundreds of years ago he foretold the coming of sheep and the railway to the highlands, spoke of the clearing of the glens, and the digging of the Caledonian Canal through the centre of Scotland. But the Brahan Seer did not see his unique ability as a gift at all; 'the sight' was something that he considered an affliction. And sometimes he was frightened by what he saw.

In time the local people grew afraid of him too. One evening they bound him with ropes, and carried him off to the beach near Rosemarkie, on the south shore of the Black Isle. There, they put out his eyes before they burned him.

Fields of wheat and barley change to pastures of sheep, and enclosures with row upon row of potatoes. A herd of rambunctious bullocks charges up to a gate to stare as I walk past. They follow me down the lane, until, fed up with their attentions, I stop and face them over the barbed-wire fence. They gaze back dumbly, not backing away. A boy rides past on a mountain bike, and dawdles back and forth across the empty road.

The country lane empties eventually onto the main road which runs from Inverness to Dingwall. The road is busy with cars, and each one conjures up a miniature whirlwind of dust as it bowls past. I have to walk down this busy highway for half a mile before I come to a short-cut I can take across the fields. It's a jarring contrast to the peace of the country lane I've just left.

When I'm across the Conon river bridge I clamber down a steep bank to a wheat field, and work along the fence, treading down thistles and stinging nettles, until I reach a levee beside the river. But there are two levees, one on either side of a stream that's rushing between steep, muddy banks overgrown with wild vegetation. I fight my way along the top of the first levee, through gorse and brambles, searching for a place to cross. In minutes I'm torn and bleeding, and stung by nettles.

At length I come to a place where the stream is narrow enough to jump, and slide down the bank onto a tiny corner of mud. Frightened, small, brown fish dart about the stream. My boots sink in past their uppers and I have to leap right away before I slide in the water. My jump lands me on a tiny, muddy shore, and I grab a handful of pretty purple flowers on the bank to steady myself. The flowers break away in my hand, and let out a sweet, pungent scent of mint. For a moment I totter on the edge of disaster, until a tuft of long grass takes my weight. I feel like MacGregor at Killiecrankie.

A path runs from here across a corner of bullrush-covered marsh to the top of another levee, where the ground is firm. This bank curves along the line of the Conon River towards mudflats and salt grasses, lining fields of sheep and cows on the one side, and sheltering marsh birds on the other. Dingwall rises out of the barley fields ahead; home for the moment.

The New World

The Immigrant

"Emigration, from a word of the most cheerful
import, came to sound most dismally in my ear.
There is nothing more agreeable to picture and
nothing more pathetic to behold. The abstract
idea, as conceived at home, is hopeful and adven-
turous . . ."

—Robert Louis Stevenson
The Amateur Immigrant

After the lights went down and the other passengers wrapped
themselves in blankets and went to sleep I cried quietly to
the rhythm of the engines, my thoughts full of the people,
and the hills and streets I'd left behind. I was sure I'd never
see any of them again. It was an enormous thing, this—this
emigration to a faraway country where I didn't know anyone
at all. There was no going back. Scotland was already a thou-

sand miles behind me, a place I'd abandoned as a country without prospects, where the only way ahead was to wait forever to fill dead men's boots. I was too impatient for that, and so I'd left my family and my friends . . . for what? I didn't know.

It was cold in Winnipeg when we landed—January cold, prairie cold—cold like nothing I'd ever experienced before. The air was raw as emery-paper, with an outside temperature of minus thirty-five degrees. The first breath I took at the top of the aircraft steps knifed into my lungs long before I felt the cold on my skin. I had to catch the rail to stop myself stumbling.

By the time we reached Vancouver it was eleven o'clock at night, a Monday night. I'd expected some kind of welcome, perhaps a small committee: an immigration officer at least, offering congratulations and a certificate or something, and directions on where to go that first night I was to spend in Canada. But no one was there, no one to recognise the great gamble I'd taken.

> *In welcoming you to Canada your Immigration Officer takes particular pride in the fact that the services he provides have assisted the newcomer to adjust to his new environment . . .*
>
> destination—CANADA

A voice on the loudspeaker interrupted my wanderings through the empty air terminal. "The last bus for downtown leaves the terminal in five minutes." I found the big blue and white, round-backed bus parked outside.

"Where are you going, son?" asked the driver as I climbed in.

"I don't know. Where do you go?"

He looked at me. "Downtown."

"Are there any hotels there?"

"Yes."

There was no traffic. The bus threaded through suburbs, along wide, empty streets lined with thick wooden telephone poles which leaned crookedly, like tired sentinels. Power lines ran haphazardly up and down and across the streets at all angles, untidy in the streetlights.

The other passengers got off the bus one by one, until I was the only one left. It started to rain. I clung to the warmth inside the bus and the doubtful security of the driver, knowing this little refuge was eroding as the buildings grew taller.

The driver stopped at a corner in the centre of the city. "This is it," he said, turning in his seat. "This is as far as I go. The bus station's just round the corner." He waited for me to get up. Rain streaked the windows.

"My bag," I said.

Reluctantly the driver stood up, opened the door, and climbed down onto the pavement. He tugged at the storage door in the side of the bus with a little T-key, and hauled my suitcase out onto the sidewalk.

"Know any hotels near here?" I asked, half-hoping that he might offer me a bed at his house. He seemed like a nice man. So far, he was the only person I knew in Canada.

He looked at me, and screwed up his eyes against the slanting rain. He nodded down the street in the direction the bus was pointing.

"Down that way," he said. "They're cheaper down by the water."

It was a good suggestion. I only had a hundred dollars in my pocket, and it would have to last me until I got a job and earned some more money. I picked up my bag, and crossed the road. The sign said W. Georgia Street. I wondered who W. Georgia was. Next to it another sign read Burrard Street, pointing back the way we'd come.

I crossed W. Georgia Street and walked down the hill. Distant lights faded in and out of the rain. In the blackness I couldn't see any water, but I could smell the damp, and a flavour of diesel and creosote on the wind.

A man staggered out of the darkness towards me. I stopped.

"Excuse me," I said. It was well past midnight. "Do you know if there's a cheap hotel anywhere near here?"

The man stopped and regarded me with half closed eyes. Not knowing what to expect I put my bag down. You never knew with strangers. He was shorter than I was, but I'd met enough North Sea fishermen to know that didn't mean anything. He swayed back and forth in the wind. When he spoke his voice was thick with drink.

"Aye," he said gravely, and the accent was pure Glasgow. "Ah ken a guid hotel. S'jist doon the road." With a great effort he turned to face back the way he'd come. "Doon there." He pointed down the hill. "Pender Street. Turn right an' it's jist on yer left. The Abbotsford. Sir Walter Scott an' a' that."

I thanked him and turned away.

"Jist come have ye'?" he shouted after me. "Jist aff the boat are ye?"

"The 'plane," wondering how he knew.

"'S'a gran' country this," he called, pulling his collar tight around his neck as the wind snatched at his words. "Ah

136

hope it's as guid tae ye as it's bin tae me." Then he was gone, passing through the streetlight and into the night.

The Abbotsford was right where the Glasgow man had said it would be. An elderly woman in a worn ochre and black uniform was sitting behind a desk in the lobby, reading a magazine.

"Yes, we've got a room," she said. "It'll be fifteen dollars. You'll have to pay in advance." She took my money and handed me a key. "The elevator's over there." She pointed down the lobby.

The room was tiny and spare, with a window that looked onto the wall of a building a few feet away. There was only a bed and a chair, and a worn, patterned carpet on the floor. But I was too tired to care. In minutes I was fast asleep.

At fifteen dollars a night, I calculated the next morning, my hundred dollars wouldn't last a week. The Abbotsford, cheap and unattractive as it was, was far too rich for my wallet. Going by the bus driver's advice, I wasn't yet close enough to the water.

Leaving my suitcase with hard-won permission at the Abbotsford, I set off in search of even seedier parts of town. They were not hard to find. The rain had stopped and the city was as full of Tuesday morning bustle as any European seaport.

The dark waters of Burrard Inlet lapped at grimy black wharves, and at the barges moored at the foot of Burrard Street. Hastings Street struck eastwards past the Canadian National Railway terminal. Soon I was passing derelict men standing in doorways, some even lying full length on the pavement. On Abbott Street I came upon the Seaman's Mission, and a ragged line of men waiting patiently for the front door to open. Across the road, a neon sign blinked at the corner of Wharf Street: *Hotel*. On the door beneath it a small hand-written notice stated "Rooms To Rent". I went in.

The lobby was nothing more than a short stretch of hallway, with a torn linoleum floor. A battered wooden counter sported the scars of Saturday night boots. A little man with thin hair and a striped shirt watched me warily from a chair.

"Yes?" It was neither harsh nor welcoming, but it was very careful.

"How much are the rooms?" I asked.

He looked me up and down. "Bathroom or not?"

"It doesn't matter."

"No bathroom, single room. Thirty-five dollars a week. No bathroom, shared room. Fifteen dollars a week."

I thought about this for a minute. Then, "Can I have a look at the rooms please?"

It was his turn to think. He wasn't used to guests who wanted to inspect the premises. He turned round and selected two keys from an upright wooden box hanging on the wall behind him. He set off up a flight of bare stairs. I followed.

The single room looked out onto a brick wall. There were no pictures on the walls, no radio, no bedside light, one curtain. It was cold and uninviting. At thirty-five dollars a week, I could barely afford two weeks in there, never mind food.

"Okay," I said, thinking of nothing complimentary to say.

The man walked on down the corridor, his soft-soled shoes squeaking on the bare lino floor. He knocked on the end door and listened. There was no answer. He muttered something under his breath and turned the key in the lock.

The room's two windows looked out into a busy street. Through a gap in the buildings across the road I could see the North Shore mountains rising out of the sea. The room itself was in cheerful disarray, a plaid logging shirt flung over the back of a chair, a pair of torn trousers splayed across one of the beds. Boots and socks and underwear and towels lay about the floor. Loose change and half a dozen empty beer bottles were scattered on a small table. A black bag sat in the corner, open-zippered, with more clothes hanging out of it. The room and whoever lived in it had a kind of bright energy, and I wondered for the first time about my new roommate.

"I'll take it," I told the hotel man.

"You'll have to come downstairs to sign in," he grumbled. "Everyone's got to sign in. And you've got to pay the rent in advance. It's how we do it here." From dour he'd turned to fussy, all in a matter of seconds.

I didn't meet my new roommate until late in the day. Feeling jet-lagged, I was taking a nap in the afternoon when the door burst open. A big man stood stock still in the doorway, contemplating me stretched out on one of the beds.

"Hi," he said at last. Then he stepped into the room and stuck out his hand. "I'm Ivor."

Like the rest of him, his hand was enormous. I shook it.

"Didn't manage to make it back here last night somehow," he said, scratching his head. "Hell of a thing."

His name was Ivor Skogheim, and he was curly-blonde with a square, planed face and puffy blue eyes. He told me he worked up north as a tree faller, lived most of the time in a logging camp. The workdays were long; every six or eight weeks he took his pay and came down to the city. Loggers were paid well, he said, hundreds of dollars a week. But when he came down to Vancouver he rarely lasted more than six or seven days before he was broke again, and ready for the trip north. He was only a year or two older than me.

"Yuh can't stay in Vancouver without money," Ivor explained. Last night he'd spent two or three hundred dollars. He was going to play it smarter this time though, he said. He'd given some of his money to his buddy Bill to look after. This time he was going to break the cycle by staying in the city for a month; maybe find a different job. There were no women in the logging camps. He liked women; he wanted to settle down with one.

I spent the week scanning the newspapers, and visiting Canada Manpower, trying to find a job. Vancouver's public transport systems were nowhere near as decipherable as the ones in Europe, and I wasted a lot of time wandering lost around the Fraser Valley and suburban Richmond, and missed a couple of interviews. At night in my lumpy bed on Water Street I found myself dreaming of home, falling in and out of sleep on the cadences of Ivor's snores, wondering if it really could have been bad enough in Scotland to drive me away.

I'm at the Distillers Company's main plant, at South Queensferry, about ten miles north of Edinburgh. It's my first day at my first job. I've been posted into the bottling hall. I'm eighteen.

The floor manager comes to me and says, "JB wants to see you in his office." He gives me a quizzical look. "You must be important, or something."

"Who's JB?" I ask.

"The managing director," says the floor manager. "We never see him down here. His office is on the top floor. You get the lift over there in the corner and take it up to the fourth floor, then you get out and turn a corner and get into another lift, and that takes you up to his office."

It's a relief to get away from the incessant, clattering noise of the bottling hall, and the pervasive smell of stale whisky. The bottling hall is a great cavern of a place, where bottles are carried down eight long, parallel conveyor belts to be filled, corked, labelled, stamped, sealed and finally boxed. Eight huge vats stand against the back wall of the great hall. Six of them are full of whisky; two are loaded with gin. These tanks are connected to the bottling 'tables' by a complicated series of lines, pipes, hoses and valves. Three hundred and twenty-five women carry out the bottling and packing operations. Only six men work in the bottling hall, providing supervision, maintenance, and technical support.

The women are tough. They range in age from sixteen to sixty. Some of them are probably older. Most of them come from the small, rough mining towns up and down the Forth Valley; places like Bo'ness, Bathgate, Kirkliston, and Winchburgh. All of them have to wear a kind of brown, sexless, wrap-around smock at work, although some of them manage to turn up in a variety of 'pre-date' guises—the ones who are going out after work with a 'fella'. They come to work with strange preparations on their faces, with curlers wound tightly through hair wrapped up in high turbans. I can feel their eyes on me as soon as I walk in the door, and I know that they've sized me up right away for what I am—a complete innocent, with no idea what I'm getting myself into.

Every time they leave the building, the women are searched at the door by hard-eyed female supervisors. Management knows from experience that bottles of whisky can walk out of the hall in the voluminous folds of the women's overalls, and they take few chances of suffering such a drain on profits. But it strikes me right away as a demeaning sort of procedure, riddled with discrepancies in class and social structure.

I see later, as Christmas approaches and the company has a run of miniatures, that some of the girls help themselves while they work, often quite liberally. Bottle one— drink one . . . bottle one—drink one. Some of them have a prodigious capacity for blended whisky. It is then—two days before Christmas—when I climb up onto the narrow gangway behind the vats to change the valves from one blend to another, that I find my exit barred by half a dozen of the girls, and turning around, see another half dozen of them blocking the way on the other side.

But on this first morning, these things are in the future.

I find my way up to the managing director's office, nervous because I don't know what he wants to see me about, although I'm guessing that he probably just wants to welcome me to the company.

The elevator door opens right into his office, and I find myself facing the managing director's desk. The broad reaches of the River Forth stretch out behind him, all the way over to the Fife shore. The Great Man is writing. He doesn't look up. I step out of the elevator and wait. The doors close behind me all by themselves. After what seems like a long time, J.B. Munro looks up from the paper he's writing and stares at me.

"I hope," he says in a rich voice, "that you don't think that just because you went to school at the Edinburgh Academy and I went to George Heriot's, that you're any better than I am." He nods curtly.

I'm speechless, almost. "No," I say, clearing my throat. "Sir."

"Good," he says, "you can go now."

Low on funds and desperate for some earnings, I took a job with the Grolier Society. My first role in my new life in Canada was going to be selling encyclopaedias. About ten of us turned up for training one Wednesday morning at a dingy classroom in a rundown office block at Main and Kingsway—a busy intersection where passing traffic rattled the windows.

Our instructor's name was Larry. He was dapper and tall, with a thin moustache and a pale face. He had watery eyes and a red nose. Larry wore a silvery suit, and polished black shoes. But he had a ready wit and a quick mind, and a response for every question.

We spent the first morning listening to a lecture about the Grolier Society and the quality of its product—the encyclopaedia we were to sell, door to door.

"It's beautifully bound," sniffed Larry, rubbing his hand across the cover of one of the books. "See this? It's made of DuPont Fabricoid."

I never discovered what DuPont Fabricoid was, or what made it so special. Larry's aggressive enthusiasm scared off most of our questions. As well, despite the fact that he called it DuPont Fabricoid, I was never sure whether that was actually its name, or whether Larry had some sort of nasal New York accent which gave the name a pronunciation peculiar to him; whether in my Scots accent it should be called something else.

Ivor's friend Bill was in the class as well, and the two of us went out to a seedy sandwich bar on Main Street for lunch. Bill had put me on to the job in the first place. He was a bright fellow—a perfect counterpoint to Ivor's deceptive lethargy. To heighten the disparity between them, Bill was short and dumpy in stature, with dark hair and dark eyes. Bill lived in an apartment in Vancouver's West End, near Stanley Park.

During the afternoon session, Larry introduced us to our sales kit: a black briefcase full of charts and calculations, and fold-out pictures of encyclopaedias, showing the full set of books fanned out across a living room carpet like a deck of over-sized playing cards. One of the graph charts showed the purchasing family how to re-distribute their weekly expenses for food, housing, entertainment and transport in order to enjoy the benefits of owning Grolier's Encyclopaedia Britannica.

Larry took us carefully through all these sales aids. He seemed to have a bad cold, for he sniffed constantly, and his voice became more adenoidal as the afternoon wore on. He finished off by showing us the piggy bank. It was his favourite.

"Dis," he intoned, "is irresistible to kids." He held up a quarter between his thumb and forefinger, and dropped it into the piggy bank's slot. The coin fell into the clear plastic contraption, dribbled down holes and tinkled along circuitous channels until it eventually clanged into the money-box.

"Ya godda try and bake your presentations just before da kids go to bed," he said. "Dey love de piggy bank. I've bade bore sales because of de goddab piggy bank dan because of de goddab books."

The next morning when I arrived the other students were clustered around the locked door of the classroom. I was late and they'd already been waiting for ten minutes, but there was no sign of Larry.

"If you guys'll hoist me up," said Bill, "I can look through the fanlight and see if there's anyone inside." We lifted him up to the transom window, above the door.

"He's in there all right. He's lying on the floor. Oh Christ!" Bill stared down at us. "He's got a needle stuck in his arm." He jumped down to the floor. "Looks like he's OD'ed."

I didn't know what he was talking about. I'd never heard the phrase before. "We should call a medic," said Bill. "We can't just leave him like that."

Just then a smartly dressed woman turned up. She had luminous eyes and a face as pale as Larry's. "I'll look after him," she said quickly. "There's no need to call anyone." She took a key out of her handbag and stared at us, daring anyone to disagree.

"Well what are you waiting here for?" she said. "There's no class today. It's cancelled. You can all go."

"How long will he be sick?" someone asked, a bit timidly.

"Tomorrow. He'll be here tomorrow morning." We left.

The next morning Larry was there at the appointed time. He took us through the remainder of the course as if nothing had happened.

That evening, at six o'clock, Larry drove us out in pairs to our 'territories'. "Ya godda ged dem when they're hobe," he explained, "and they're always hobe at dinnertime." He stopped the car and let Bill and me out and told us to work as a team, down opposite sides of the same dark suburban street. I steeled myself and walked up to the first door and rang the bell. A man opened it; I told him my purpose and found myself staring at the door again—all in a matter of seconds. Across the road, Bill had the same experience.

We held a brief consultation in the middle of the deserted road. "This might not be a lot of fun," Bill whispered. We each tried another house, with similar results.

"Ya godda ged into the house," Larry had told us. "Ya can't tell theb too much on the doorsteb, otherwise ya haven't godda chance. Ya godda ged theb to invite ya in." It seemed like an impossible assignment.

The people in the third house invited me in, right inside, into their living room. They offered me a cup of coffee and they were so pleasant and polite that I thought Larry must have planted them to boost my morale. I launched into my spiel, and they were genuinely taken with the idea of owning a set of the Grolier Society's encyclopaedias.

I took them through the whole presentation, just as Larry had taught us. I unfolded the charts with their pictures and explanations and pie-graphs and showed them how the whole thing was affordable, even for a low-income family. I left the charts lying out on the living room floor as Larry had told us to do. They loved the piggy bank, and watched the coin make its way down the little plastic alleyways and drops.

They didn't flinch when I brought out the contract they'd have to sign with the Grolier Society in order to buy the whole set on time payments. When I finished, the husband went through to the kitchen to get a pen and a chequebook, while the wife explained that they were about to start a family and this was just the thing they needed. I couldn't believe it.

By the time the husband came back into the living room I knew what I had to do. I took a deep breath and told them that I couldn't let them buy the books. "I'd love to sell them to you," I said, "but I can't. I just can't. If you really want a set of encyclopaedias you should go down to one of the big bookstores in town and you can buy them there for about half the price you'll end up paying if you sign this contract."

They thanked me and gave me another cup of coffee and some cake before showing me to the door. They looked disappointed that I wouldn't let them buy the set there and then. But my conscience was clear, and I knew that I'd come to the end of my career as an encyclopaedia salesman. I'd have to find another way to survive in this strange country.

The next day was a Saturday. At lunchtime I walked up to meet Bill, and an Australian fellow from the encyclopaedia course, in the bar of the Devonshire Hotel on Georgia Street. It was our custom in Scotland to meet for a lunchtime pint on Saturdays at our favourite pub, to discuss plans for the weekend, compare sports fixtures and the addresses of Saturday night parties. It was a civilised ritual, and we never drank more than a pint or two.

The Devonshire Hotel had a semi-basement beer parlour with separate entrances for *Men* and *Ladies with Escorts*, a strange and unnatural segregation of things. It should have been a warning.

A waiter brought beer to our table in curious hourglass-shaped glasses, each glass about a third of a pint. Bill picked up a saltshaker, and sprinkled salt into his beer. It was an odd thing to do and I asked him about it. "Gets rid of the gas," he explained. "It's easier on the stomach." I decided not to try it.

Half an hour later we ordered more beer from a waiter who was circulating the room with a tray laden with over-brimming glasses. We finished making our plans for the day, and Bill and I went off to make telephone calls from the pay phones in the lobby, while Graeme, the Australian, went to the toilet. When we arrived back at our table we found it occupied by three rough-looking logger-types, who were drinking the beer we'd only just bought.

"Excuse me," I said, "there must be a mistake here. We were sitting at this table and these are our beers. I just bought them."

The loggers stared at me as if I'd just landed from the moon. "Fuck off," one of them said.

A short argument followed this, but the loggers weren't interested in negotiating. I went up to the bar and explained the situation to the barman.

"We don't want any trouble in here," said the barman mildly, "Why don't you guys just fuck off?"

I couldn't believe it. "Well . . . no," I said, annoyed now at the injustice of it. "Why on earth should we? We haven't done anything wrong."

"Look son, do you want me to call the manager?"

I told him to go ahead. The manager appeared a minute later. The barman told him that he'd ordered us to leave, and we'd refused.

"Right," said the manager, "I want you guys out of here right now."

"Wait a minute. There's a bit more to it than that," I said.

"If you don't leave right now I'm calling the police." He reached for a telephone on the counter.

"We're not leaving," said Graeme. "Not until you give us our beer, or our money back."

"Right," said the manager. He picked up the telephone.

Two minutes later, four uniformed policemen walked into the bar. "Bit early in the day for this," said one of them. It was half past twelve.

The barman said something to one of them, and the policeman immediately took hold of my arm, twisted it up behind my back and propelled me down a hallway behind the bar. Another policemen opened a pair of barred doors, and I found myself staring into the back of a blue police paddy wagon.

"Wait a minute," I heard myself saying. "Aren't you interested in what we've got to say?"

"Nope." The policeman pushed my arm further up my back, and threw me in the wagon. Seconds later, Bill and Graeme followed me in there, and the door slammed shut.

"We sure lost control of that one," muttered Bill as the paddy wagon jolted down the street.

Five minutes later, the paddy wagon backed up an alleyway and we were hustled into the back of the Main Street Police Station.

In coming to Canada, you have made an important decision—one that required courage and determination to meet the challenges associated with establishment in a new country. Possessing these characteristics,

149

it should not take you very long to become happily
settled in Canada—the country of your choice.
destination—CANADA

A constable stared coldly at us from behind a desk.

"Empty your pockets," he said. I put sixty dollars and some odds and ends on the counter top. Bill and Graeme emptied their pockets as well. The constable shovelled each pile into a separate plastic bag.

"Shoelaces and belt," he said.

"Pardon?"

"Take off your shoelaces and your belt!"

Bill poked me in the ribs. "So you don't hang yourself." There was no humour in his voice.

When that was done the desk cop took down our particulars—name, address, date of birth and the rest. When he finished, a second policeman ushered us into a wire-caged service elevator, beside two unshaven prisoners who were handcuffed to each other. The lift went up six floors, and then Bill and Graeme and I were separated.

I was taken down a long, tile-walled corridor to a scratched steel door. The gaoler took a bunch of keys from his belt, opened the door, and thrust me into a cell full of people. The cell was a big, square room with white tiled walls, and windows covered with wire mesh. An open toilet stood public and filthy in one corner. Eight, two-tiered metal bunks were stacked in the middle of the cell. More than thirty men were jammed in there and all the bunks were occupied; there was nowhere to sit. I slid down to the floor with my back against the wall, and waited to see what would happen next.

150

I didn't talk to anyone in the cell; I didn't like the look of any of the men in there. Over the next few hours gaolers came and took some of the men away, and occasionally pushed new offenders inside. A kind of pecking order evolved, with seniority related to time in the cell. I worked my way slowly around the wall, ready to take the next available bunk. One came free near the toilet bowl.

I was tired and stiff. Even though the metal bunk was no softer than the cold concrete floor I could distribute my weight along its length. I must have fallen asleep right away.

The manager tilts his wrist and looks at his watch. "Right," he says briskly. "It's like this. The woman turns up at six and she's got to be painted from head to toe." I stare at him, as if he's just sprouted rabbit ears. "It's all right," adds the manager hastily, "you don't have to do the painting. There's a make-up man for that."

I'm having difficulty following him.

"Once that's done," he goes on, "she just has to stand in the lobby in her swimming costume, and greet the punters as they file in. All you've got to do is to make sure she's there. Oh, and you'd better check that the make-up man leaves some bare skin somewhere. Not much, but if he paints her all over she'll suffocate. It's what happens in the film," he adds.

This is Dundee, a little more than a year before Vancouver city jail, but light years distant. I've been sent up here from Edinburgh to relieve the local theatre manager on his day off. Doing day-relief is my job. I'm a trainee executive with the Rank Organisation, Film and Theatre Division.

"I'm sorry," I say, "But I haven't got the foggiest idea what you're talking about."

The manager stares at me; we're standing in the ornate, marble-floored lobby of the Gaumont Theatre. "Goldfinger," he says. He waves his arm around the lobby. The place is festooned with publicity photographs and posters of Scotland's hottest film star, Sean Connery. A life-sized cardboard cut-out of Shirley Eaton gazes wanly from the box-office cubicle. Luscious and elegant, the actress is painted from head to foot in shimmering gold leaf.

"Didn't they tell you? It's the Scottish premiere." He corrects himself. "I mean the World premiere. The Odeon Leicester Square doesn't get it until tomorrow." I know the Odeon Leicester Square as a grand old theatre in the heart of London, with plush armchair seating and thick-piled carpets. It's the company's showpiece, and it hosts all the big events. Except for the premiere of Goldfinger.

"The premiere! Tonight?"

"Tonight," he says, "and I'll be late for my fishing if I don't get going right away. My pal's waiting for me on his boat at Broughty Ferry and he won't hang about all morning."

"How can you take the day off when the premiere of Goldfinger's on tonight?"

"Nervous?" He grins. I like him; he's one of the better managers. His staff is well trained and professional, his theatre always immaculate and its operations smooth whenever I come up here to relieve him. It's not like that at many of the other theatres.

"No need to be; pretty well everything's taken care of. You just have to be here to preside over it, and take the confections inventory and lock up at the end of the night." He snatches another look at his watch. "Christ, I'll miss the boat." He heads for the big glass doors at the front of the theatre.

He turns around, halfway through the door. "Oh, I nearly forgot. The Connerys will be here at seven-fifteen. There's half a dozen seats roped off for them at the front of the Upper Circle. You should escort them up there and make sure they're seated and comfortable. The curtain goes up at seven-thirty. I don't think there's anything else." Then he's gone, a man with his priorities in order.

The evening is just as he said it would be. The woman turns up at six o'clock with a make-up man, and is duly embossed with gold paint before she takes up her stance in the lobby. Rather than greet the audience as they arrive though, she stands motionless and wooden, like a Parisienne street-mime artist, and people peer at her to see if she's real. The Connerys turn up punctually at seven-fifteen—Sean's mother and father, and his brother Neil—but there's no sign of the star himself. "He's away shooting another film," says his brother as I show them to their seats.

I woke up with a jump, to find a hand running up my leg towards my private parts. In a reflex I lashed out with my foot and connected with the man's face. It was a lucky shot. Blood spurted from his nose over my jeans and he flung himself backwards and cracked his head against the wall. I jumped to my feet, half awake, dimly prepared to fight. I'd read stories about the rules in jail—be tough or go under.

I stood over him, wondering whether to hit him again. But he'd banged his head so hard against the tile wall that his eyes were glazed. Blood was gushing from his nose onto his shirt and his teeth were open in a kind of grimace. For a second I felt sorry for him, and then the metal observation plate in the cell door slammed back and one of the gaolers looked in. The door whipped open right away and the gaoler grabbed me with both hands. Before I knew what was happening I was outside in the corridor. The door slammed shut behind me.

"Boy, you're in real trouble now," he breathed, his face too close to mine. "Fighting in the cells. They'll throw the book at you for that." He took a handful of my shirt and pulled me down the corridor behind him.

The gaoler's office was at the far end of the corridor, and he dragged me all the way down there.

"Take him downstairs for prints," said the man who was sitting inside, after the gaoler explained what he'd seen.

The gaoler took me down a set of narrow back stairs to a small laboratory.

A man in a white lab coat stood up when we came in. The gaoler left us alone. The technician seemed like a sympathetic man, but he hardly spoke at all.

"When can I get out of here?" I asked him. "I don't know what I'm supposed to have done."

The technician looked at me sadly, and pushed a mini paint-roller across a blacked metal plate, like something we used to do when we made woodcuts at school.

"They all say that," he said.

"What?"

"None of them seem to know why they're in here. None of them have done anything."

My stomach sank, but at least the technician had referred to 'they' and not 'you'. It slowly began to dawn on me that no one in here had any authority to let me out. No one had any authority to do anything except keep me here, and I knew that the technician was right; that this was a place where everyone proclaimed their innocence whether it was true or not. Nobody believed anyone else, and nothing—except for the coarseness of the place—was taken at face value. The system had a life of its own.

"Well then, do you know when can I post bail?" I asked. "Isn't that what you get to do?"

He took the fingers of my right hand and rolled them one by one, first on the inky metal plate, then on a paper pad sectioned into squares. He did it quickly, expertly, before I knew what he was doing. He did the same with the fingers and thumb of my left hand.

"Monday," he said. "You might be able to post bail on Monday. JP's don't work on the weekends." It was Saturday evening.

"JP's? What's a JP?"

"Justice of the Peace. They set bail for you." He looked at me. "They don't work on weekends."

The injustice of it was enormous. The only people who could get me out of jail took weekends off to play golf or watch football, while I stayed in jail. How could this be possible?

I suddenly remembered that they're not supposed to lock you up without letting you speak to a lawyer. "Don't I get a phone call or something?" I asked. "I want to speak to a lawyer. It's my right."

"Sure," he said. "Didn't they tell you?" He pushed a black telephone across the counter towards me.

"I don't have the telephone number."

He shrugged his shoulders. "There's a telephone book

over there." He pointed to a shelf in the corner of the room, and went out the door.

I didn't know any lawyers in Vancouver. I hardly knew anyone, except Bill and Ivor and Graeme. Larry didn't seem like a good bet under the circumstances. I hardly even knew the name of the hotel where I was renting the room. I opened the phone book and found that all the pages for 'Barristers and Solicitors' had been ripped out.

The technician came back into the room. "That's enough time," he said, and pushed a button. He wasn't such a nice man after all.

The gaoler came in, a heavy-set man, with a pot belly straining at his grey-blue gabardine jacket. He took me back up to the office on the top floor.

"I don't want to go back in that cell," I told him. "I was attacked in there. There are people in there who can't keep their hands to themselves."

The senior gaoler gave his colleague a sickly smile, and put on an exaggerated lisp. "We're all queerth in here aren't we Thethil," he said.

I didn't see the humour in it. "I don't care," I said, "but I'm not going back in there again."

"Right," said my escort. "Come with me." He started walking me back up the corridor.

"Wait a minute," I protested. "I want to post bail. You can't keep me in here. I haven't done anything."

The gaoler's eyes narrowed. "Fighting in the cells," he said. "That's not a bad start."

"But I haven't done anything to get put in here in the first place." I still didn't realise that I was wasting my breath. "I want to know what the charges are."

"Monday," said the gaoler. "You'll find that out on Monday, when the JP comes in."

He opened a door and followed me into a lockup containing eight smaller cells, each one fronted by vertical steel bars. The gaoler unlocked one of the doors and slid it back. "In here," he said, and turned round and went out, slamming the door behind him.

A man was inside the cell, pacing up and down like a caged animal at the zoo. He only had room for two steps before he had to turn round again. It was a tiny cell, with two bunks, one on top of the other. The man marched back and forth, back and forth. I felt a desperate need to lie down, but there was a madness in my new companion and I was afraid of picking the wrong bunk.

"Wasn't me that did it," the man was muttering over and over. He paid no attention to me at all. "I didn't put her in there. Wasn't me." After a few minutes he seemed to notice my presence in his cell. "I didn't put her in there," he insisted, and his eyes scanned me wildly. I thought him quite mad.

"Where?" I asked, although I didn't really want to know.

He stopped pacing and stared at me. "The hospital."

"What's the matter with her?" I asked to humour him.

"I didn't hit her," he said. "It wasn't me stuck it in there. I gotta get with her for the operation."

"What operation," I asked as sympathetically as I could.

He stared at me as if I was an idiot. "To get it out," he said. "They gotta get the axe out, eh?"

Minutes ticked painfully by as my new cellmate's story unravelled in a graphically inarticulate way. His wife was in

157

hospital for an emergency operation to remove an axe from her back. He said he hadn't put it there, but I didn't think I should ask him who had, or what her chances of survival were. Instead I asked him which bunk was his.

Each bunk had a horsehair mattress and a thin grey military-style blanket. They were more comfortable than the bunks in the other cell, but barely. Our cell even had its own seat-less toilet bowl, and a small washbasin. But there was no privacy; everyone had to perform their ablutions in full view of everyone else in the little complex of cells.

Renfield Street is packed solid with people. I fight my way through the crowd to the stage door and bang on it with my fist. Jimmy Murray is already inside. Jimmy is training in Aberdeen along with me, but he's drawn the short straw up there. He gets to work at the Odeon with Mr. Prior, an austere, humourless, church-going man. But Jimmy's straw is only slightly shorter than the one I've pulled. I have to work with Mr. Aitken at the Gaumont, on busy Union Street. Mr. Aitken is the spitting image of a World War Two fighter pilot, complete with the handlebar moustache, and all the bluster of someone who has never known one end of a Spitfire from the other. Mr. Aitken is a born showman who should have had a stable of artistes to manage, a carny barker without a carnival. But Mr. Aitken is usually paralytic by 9 o'clock each evening, and I have to stay on until the theatre empties every night to make sure everything is properly closed up. Mr. Aitken survives in the theatre business because his faithful secretary Queenie is always on hand to pack him off home in a taxi if there is the slightest sign that anyone from head office might turn up to inspect his operation.

"They can only get three thousand people in here," Jimmy explains when I'm safely inside the theatre. "All these punters outside want in, but they haven't got tickets."

"They seem to be getting quite wound up about it," I tell him. The crowd stretches for blocks, filling the surrounding streets, stopping the traffic.

The theatre manager explains what he wants us to do. A security man stands at his side. About thirty of us trainee managers have been drafted in from all over Scotland and the north of England to help run the evening's event, a gala live show with the Beatles—as it turns out, one of the last live shows they'll ever do indoors in Britain.

"You've got tae keep the wimmen off them," explains the security man when the manager has finished. "Stop them frae stormin' the stage."

Both Jimmy and I are over six feet tall, and so we're directed to stand right in front of the stage, facing the audience, with our backs to the performance.

"We've got time to nip across the road for a pint before the show," says Jimmy, checking his watch. "There's a good hour yet."

We check with the bruiser at the stage door so that he'll recognise us when we return, then let ourselves out into the crowd, and force our way across the street. The crowd is thicker than ever, but the bar opposite is surprisingly empty. We sit up at the counter and order beer. A young woman slides into a seat next to us at the bar, a dark-eyed, brown-skinned girl. She glances at us.

"You with the show?" she asks, eyeing the tuxedos that all Rank's management people have to wear. Her voice is cool, her accent unmistakeably American. She's barely in her twenties.

159

"Yes." We introduce ourselves. She tells us her name is Mary Wells, and we realise that she's one of the stars in the show—she'll be singing on stage just before the Beatles. She's just had a big hit in Britain and the United States called "My Guy", and she is quite lovely, with a level of assurance and sophistication we're not used to finding in a woman who's virtually the same age as we are. We don't know what to say to her at first; don't know how to speak with someone like this from another world, sitting with us in a Glasgow bar.

Our beer arrives and Mary says, "I'll get them. I'd like to buy the drinks. Everyone's been very kind to me since I came here."

Neither of us realise then just how big a star Mary is in the United States. She was one of the first singers to bring an evocative mix of folk and gospel and blues to popular attention, and many consider her the true founder of the famous Motown sound. She's a close collaborator of the legendary Smokey Robinson, and the Beatles have specifically invited her to tour with them. But Mary doesn't say anything about these things; she doesn't speak about herself at all. Her gentle humility and interest in her surroundings opens us up, and we pass half an hour with her, talking about the United States, about Detroit where she's from, about ourselves. She's unusually unassuming for someone in the theatre business, but when Jimmy and I compare notes later, we both find that we're left with a small, almost imperceptible impression of sadness about her, an air of loneliness. We put it down to homesickness.

When it's time to go back to the theatre we push our way to the stage door, shielding Mary from the crowd. There's a smell of burning in the air, and the crowd is crammed across the street, from one side to the other. We hear the sound of breaking glass from somewhere nearby. A parked car has been rolled on its side and set on fire. Police and Fire bells fill the air, and the Glasgow polis move in on horseback to patrol the street and push the people back.

It's just as wild inside the theatre. The Stalls and the Dress Circle are overflowing with young girls. There's hardly a man in the place. Jim and I move out and take up our stations in front of the stage, to the right of centre, at the foot of one of the main aisles.

Sounds Incorporated are the leadoff group. They come on stage, and they're good. Not every group plays well live; some of them are simply products of the recording studio. Sounds Inc. are better than most, but not quite as good as their records.

Mary comes on when they're finished, and sings with a voice full of character and soul. She is lovely and talented, but somehow out of place in this setting, with an audience of crazy girls who only want to hear the Beatles.

Then the Beatles come on, the four of them bouncing onto the stage, with John Lennon in the lead. They pick up their instruments, and the place erupts. Young women flood into the aisles and surge in a wave towards the stage. The Beatles begin to play. The screaming starts and we're right in the middle of it; a thin, black line in our monkey suits, standing in no man's land between the stage and three thousand frenzied women.

The Beatles launch right in to "A Hard Day's Night". And the songs come belting out without a break. "If I Fell In Love With You", "Eight Days A Week", "She Loves Me", and the others. The sound man cranks up the volume to combat the noise of the screaming, and the women charge down on the stage like a manic tide, and fling themselves, weeping and crying and screaming, at our thin wall of defenders. The Edinburgh Academy never prepared me for this.

The Beatles are good—very good—far better live than they are on record. The sound they make is extraordinary. It blasts out of massive speaker stacks that reach up to the proscenium, and I find myself staggering under the onslaught, temporarily unbalanced by it.

I catch one girl and try to push her back up the aisle, and four more launch themselves at me. They climb over the seats, and throw themselves over the top of the other patrons like a medieval horde, while the Beatles play on, moving seamlessly from one song into another, each one sending the audience into fresh paroxysms of ecstasy and hysteria. Girls further back who can't reach the stage begin to throw things; combs, lipstick, and pieces of underwear sail over our heads, onto the stage. Lennon kicks a brassiere back into the audience, laughs, and plays on.

We try linking arms for a few minutes, but it's hopeless. The women burrow under us, try to climb over us, dart between our legs, threaten to overwhelm us with a crush of massed bodies. I catch two more of them, one on each arm, and struggle to hold station. The music powers on, louder and louder, the volume so high that I'm starting to feel dizzy, the heat excruciating under the lights. But I know that if I fall down I'll be trampled.

The Beatles change to a softer instrumental piece from "A Hard Day's Night". Another girl flings herself at me in an effort to reach the stage. She is utterly distraught, weeping uncontrollably, her face and hair wet with tears. She falls against me, too exhausted now to scream. I hold on like death, and suddenly she relaxes. "Oh, this is nice," she says. Her eyes close and she holds my arms about her and rocks backwards and forwards. I catch a glimpse of Jimmy beside me, his bow tie askew, one sleeve of his jacket torn off. Two girls are beating at his chest and face with clenched fists, trying to climb over him onto the stage. He looks as though he's been in a Glasgow brawl. Except that there is lipstick on his cheek, and a huge grin on his face.

It goes on like this for an hour, and then the show is over. I feel like a piece of blotting paper, saturated and then wrung out. But we'd all been invited at the briefing for post-show drinks upstairs in the theatre restaurant, and now we're just about ready for it. After the curtain comes down we wait until the theatre is empty, and nothing is left onstage except for the speaker stacks, and Ringo's drum kit.

We find that the madness has shifted backstage; it's pandemonium, as if half the fans from the front of the house have somehow found their way to the back of the theatre. Paul, Ringo, George and then John push their way through the crowd, and sweep two steps at a time up the wide staircase, Lennon making faces and tossing out quips. Girls grab at the Beatles' clothes, trying to tear off souvenirs. Jimmy and I muscle our way through the crush, and climb the stairs. Everyone is packed like pilchards into a huge room. The Beatles are at the front, guzzling cakes and hors d'oeuvres, but we find ourselves stuck at the back behind a sea of heads. We each grab a bottle of Carlsberg and look around for Mary Wells, but we can't see her in the crush. So we hang around for as long as it takes us to drink the beer, and then we head off in search of a pub.

It's the night before my twentieth birthday, the night I take a drink with the Beatles. It seems like a long time ago.

℘

163

A scream woke me up in the middle of the night. It pierced the silent cells and chilled my blood, and sat me up straight in my bunk. A few seconds later another scream rang out, and then another and another. The screaming went on and on; I thought it would never end. After a while the screams ran together, plaintive and primitive, reverberating through the bars of the cell like a tuning fork, tingling deep into the roots of my hair. I pulled the blanket over my head, but there was no escape from it. In the end the screams died away to isolated whimperings, and then they stopped.

A gaoler brought me cold toast and lukewarm tea in the morning. Ten minutes later he came back and called out my name.

"Here," I answered.

"Come with me," he said, unlocking the cell door.

We went down the corridor, and as we did we passed an enormous man in a bright red logging jacket. The man could barely walk; he was being helped by two gaolers who were half dragging, half carrying him. He was a frightening sight, his face smashed and bloody, his eyes slitted between torn, distended eyebrows and grotesquely swollen cheekbones. His nose had been beaten half inside his head, his clothes torn to ribbons and soaked in so much blood that it was impossible to tell the original colour of the material. He wasn't making any sound at all, but he must have been the man who was screaming in the night.

My gaoler took me down in the elevator to the main lobby. Ivor was standing by the big doors that led out to Main Street. Bill and Graeme were standing with him. The gaoler took me up to the counter where we'd been checked in the day before.

"Here, sign for these," said the constable behind the desk, emptying the bits and pieces from my pockets, and my belt and shoelaces out of a bag.

I checked the list. Everything was there except that only fifteen dollars was listed as cash.

"I'm not signing for this," I said, "I had sixty dollars in my wallet when I came in here. I'm not signing for anything until it's all there." It was all the money I had.

The desk constable's face flushed. The gaoler with me spoke his name softly, "Wally . . ."

Wally reached down below the counter. "Must've fallen out," he muttered, and brought up a small sheaf of bank notes from a shelf under the desk.

I counted the notes. There was sixty dollars exactly, and some change from my pocket. I signed the sheet, threaded the laces into my shoes, and hooked my belt through the loops in my trousers.

Ivor had brought Bill's car, which he'd parked on Main Street. He drove us to Bill's apartment in the West End and we brewed up fresh coffee. I went out onto the balcony and looked out at Stanley Park and the North Shore mountains. The air was fresh and clean and it seemed to me that I could fly if I wanted to.

"Did you hear the screaming in the night?" asked Bill. He handed me a cup of coffee.

"Yes. It woke me up. Did you find out what it was about?"

"It happened in my cell," said Bill. "They brought in this big longshoreman just after midnight. He was so drunk he couldn't stand up, so they just poured him into the cell and he collapsed on the floor. I had one of the top bunks and I was more or less asleep, so I was only just aware of it at first.

"About an hour after that they brought in two junkies they'd picked up somewhere. One of them tripped over the longshoreman and swore at him and gave him a kick. The big guy never moved; he was out of it. After a while the junkies started yelling for medication, and eventually one of the gaolers came along and gave them some pills. They swallowed the pills and this got them all hopped up. One of them said he was going to teach the big guy a lesson for getting in his way. So he gave the longshoreman a kick, and then another. He started getting really worked up about it, and kicked him again and again. The longshoreman tried to get up and defend himself, but the junkie kicked him in the face and wouldn't quit. He was getting hurt real bad, and that's when the screaming started.

"It went on for a long time." Bill shook his head, as if he still couldn't believe what he'd seen. "That junkie kicked the living shit out of the big guy's head and the guy screamed and couldn't defend himself and no one came to help him."

"Why didn't someone in the cell try to stop it?" I asked.

"Are you kidding? Those guys would've killed anyone who got in the way. I just kept my eyes shut and tried to pretend I wasn't there." Bill shook his head again. "You should have seen that longshoreman in the morning. There was more of his face on his jacket than there was left on his head."

I told him I'd seen the man in the corridor.

"It's amazing that he wasn't killed," said Ivor.

Hester had told me I'd come here—more or less. Hester was an usherette at the Odeon theatre in Edinburgh when I worked there. She had the gift of healing by touch, and she could read tea leaves. Gina, the little Italian girl who worked on tickets, told me that Hester could see things that other people couldn't see; that she had the second sight. Gina said that Hester could see your 'aura', and tell from that what was going to happen to you. Hester was always trying to line me up with Gina.

Gina was more impressionable than I was. But it was true that Hester had read Dreama's tea leaves, and had told her that she was going to have an accident. Dreama was the Greek woman who ran the ice cream concession in the theatre lobby. Two days later she was knocked down by a cement truck in front of the theatre and broke both her legs. We had to hire a temp for the next two months to sell ice cream.

Hester would study the leaves in the bottom of my teacup, and then take my face in her old hands and gaze into my eyes for a long time, boring right into me with her deep, brown eyes. It would make my head tingle with energy, as if she was transferring a current. "You're going away," she said to me one day. "A long way away; across the sea."

"Will I come back?" I never knew whether to take Hester seriously. With her wizened face, lined, leathery skin and long tar-black hair, she had the look of a gypsy. She could have been forty-five or sixty-five; it was impossible to tell how old she was.

"No," she said, "not really."

A few days after we got out of jail, Ivor ran out of money, and announced that he was going up north, back to the woods. There were no decent jobs in the paper for me, and the lines of derelicts waiting for food every day at the Salvation Army Mission across from the Dominion Hotel were a depressing sight: a constant reminder that I'd be joining them if I didn't earn some money soon.

Vancouver Island

Walking across Granville Street Bridge one sunny morning I asked Bill about the mountains I could see in the distance. They seemed to float hazily above the ocean, like a kind of never-never land. It was a crisp morning and there was a mellow sharpness in the air, as if spring was not far away. The distant mountains looked mysterious and inviting.

"That's Vancouver Island," said Bill. "It's nice over there . . . it's an easy-going sort of place."

Back at the hotel, I rummaged through my bag and dug out a telephone number. John Lawrence, Duncan, Vancouver Island. I'd known his daughter in Scotland; she was the main reason I'd come to Canada's west coast. She'd talked to me about Vancouver Island, painted it in vivid colours, and filled me with ideas about opportunities that would never arise in Scotland. I found a telephone.

John's voice on the telephone was warm and cheerful. "I've heard of you," he said when I introduced myself. "I thought you might call one of these days. There's a bed for you here in our guest cottage if you want it. When are you coming over?"

It sounded too good to be true. I told him I'd come over on the ferry, on the weekend.

A lush green field sloped down from John's guest cottage to a lake. Sheep nibbled at the grass. On the other side of the lake, Mount Prevost lifted its twin tops into a blue sky. Birds sang and the sun shone.

The little green-painted guest cottage had a cosy room with a bed, an oil stove, and a small bathroom. John lived in the main house a few yards away. Altogether he had about a dozen acres of pastoral property off the winding country road which runs between Duncan and Maple Bay. After the chaos of Vancouver the place was an embrocation to the spirit.

Cowichan was a place where it wasn't difficult to draw connections across a hundred years; a leafy, pastoral valley, silvered with its own culture and history, rooted by the towering cedar and Douglas fir trees across its hillsides. It had a permanence that couldn't have changed much from the days of its pioneer settlers, and after the setbacks of the first few weeks it re-kindled my enthusiasm for Canada. I went back to Vancouver for a few days, then packed up my things and moved over to the Island.

Living on the Island was altogether different from the mainland. Vancouver Island is more than three hundred miles long, and when I arrived there, the top half of it was still unconnected by road to the bottom half. With a population of no more than half a million people, on an island almost as big as England, there was plenty of room to explore.

Two days after I moved over from Vancouver I was hired to work in an agricultural feeds plant, just south of the silver bridge in Duncan. It was my job to stack hundredweight sacks of meal in the shed, load up a big flatbed truck, and deliver feed and supplies to farms up and down the Cowichan and Koksilah Valleys. A week later I was shown how to work the mechanical shovel, and set to work unloading bran cars parked on a spur of the E & N Railway line behind the plant.

It was hard, unrelenting work. The mechanical shovel had a mind of its own, and kept burrowing into the shifting bran, dragging me down into a suffocating, porous dustiness. It was like trying to move quicksand; I couldn't keep my feet, and my boots filled up with the stuff.

The men at the plant tossed hundredweight sacks around like rag dolls. They never took breaks for coffee, or anything except a short lunch. When they finished one job they went off to look for another one. Coming from Britain, where the work day was punctuated with frequent tea and cigarette breaks, this was hard for me to understand. These Canadians were tough and conscientious. I couldn't believe how hard they worked. I looked forward to the short lunchtime break, when I'd climb up a ladder on the south wall of the building, and sit with my sandwiches on a tiny platform high above the railway line which snaked across the flats to the forest line at the edge of the valley. Some days I was so tired I fell asleep up there, with my legs dangling over a fifty-foot drop.

At the end of the day I could hardly drag myself down Maple Bay Road to the little cottage by the lake. "If everyone in this country works as hard as this I don't know how long I can survive," I told John. But slowly, as I worked myself into shape and my body adjusted to the pace, the job became easier.

Then I came down with a mysterious illness. Joe Tassin, the local doctor, was called in to have a look at me. Joe was a stocky man who spoke in a slow, measured drawl, and he looked as if he could have been Mark Twain's brother. He checked me over carefully, lifted up my eyelids, and listened to my chest through his stethoscope.

"Chickenpox," he said, stepping back from the side of the bed.

"It can't be chickenpox. I'm twenty-one. Only children get chickenpox."

Dr. Tassin lifted one of his eyebrows. "Ever had chickenpox?"

"No. I've had mumps and measles though."

"Well you've got chickenpox. It doesn't matter how old you are. If you haven't had it you can get it." He scribbled out a prescription. "I'll get someone to drop this off for you. But you're in quarantine now," he said, "for two weeks."

He was a kind man, Doc Tassin, easy going and soft spoken, with thoughtful brown eyes, and a small moustache. Perhaps he thought I needed a rest from work. But despite the lassitude induced by the chickenpox, I wanted to get fit again, to get on with my new life.

Just as the chickenpox was coming to an end I saw a cabin advertised for rent, a few miles down the road in Maple Bay. It was on Chisholm Trail, a small, brown cabin with a shingle roof. The front deck looked over Maple Bay to the sharp cliff face of Mount Maxwell on Saltspring Island, and the morning sunrise. Inside, the walls were made of heavy, compressed cardboard. But the cabin was clean and simple, and, at forty dollars a month, the price was right. I took it.

Before the chickenpox struck I'd been to the pulp mill at Crofton for an interview, and I'd filled out an employment application form. The BC Forest Products mill there was reckoned to be the best place in the valley to work, because the working conditions were good and it paid higher wages than anywhere else. Now I received a call from the personnel office offering me a job in the bleach plant, so I handed in my notice to the manager at the feeds and fertilisers plant.

The Mill

The mill sat on about fifty acres of shore land, and I saw it for the first time as I drove down the hill into the village of Crofton. A ferry, looking like a small beetle beneath the dark bulk of Maple Mountain, was making its way across the water to Vesuvius on Saltspring Island. Beyond the ferry the Gulf Islands were scattered perfect and green up the inside coast of Vancouver Island. It seemed to me that, except for the smoke stacks at the mill, the scene must have looked much the same when Captain Vancouver came this way nearly two hundred years earlier.

I was put to work in the bleach plant, where the raw pulp came down big pipes from the digester cookers to be washed and cleaned to an oatmeal white. The bleach plant was a huge building; in fact it consisted of two big buildings side by side, and four storeys high.

The operators in there had to keep a close rein on their temperatures and chemical mixtures. If they didn't, things began to go wrong. Wrong could go all the way to a dangerous chlorine leak if someone overdid things or tweaked the wrong knobs. My main job was to clean up the messes the operators made when they made mistakes.

"Big spill downstairs," said Al Charles, the first night I was there.

"Where?"

"Dunno," he said. "You'll have to go down and look for it. It might be on the ground floor, but work your way down from here. You'll know when you find it."

I raced off down the stairs and ran through both sides of the third floor, checking in dark corners, behind tanks and motors and pipes. Everything looked fine. I shot down the next flight of stairs, and ploughed knee deep in a thick brown mass the texture of porridge.

"You just hose it down and wash it away," Al had said, so I hooked a thick hosepipe up to one of the water pipes, turned on the valve and got to work. I'd been told to be careful not to spray the electric motors in case I shorted them out. When I finished I turned off all the valves, drained the hoses and coiled them up.

Life at the mill was uncomplicated. The pay was good—three or four times what I could have earned in Scotland. Four or five tour foremen hung around the bleach plant during the day, so it was necessary to look busy. But the afternoon and graveyard shifts only had one foreman—and he stayed in his office most of the time. The crew I was working with seemed competent, and on some shifts there was hardly anything for me to do. But I was beginning to hear stories about the steam plant, which made me nervous.

The steam plant lay over on the other side of the mill. I never went there unless I absolutely had to—to deliver something, or collect a piece of equipment. The steam plant was where they concocted the cooking liquors that were used to process the wood chips. The place stank, and the guys who worked in there were all filthy. They slouched around in soiled, blackened overalls, and wore yellow hard hats with big perspex visors, and black gloves, and heavy rubber boots on their feet. Sometimes you'd see one of them wearing oxygen breathing apparatus and hoses, looking like an alien. The guys from the steam plant didn't speak to anyone from the other parts of the mill, and sat together as a group in the canteen.

I bumped into one of them in the Maple Bay Inn one night. Bill turned up in a big green Beaumont roadster with shiny chrome all round its front, and white-walled tires. He had spots on his face and looked years younger in regular clothes than he did in his steam plant outfit.

"Wouldn't work anyplace else in the whole goddammed mill," he said, pouring tomato juice into his beer.

"Not even newsprint?" Everyone tried to get a job in newsprint. Nothing ever went wrong in there. It was the cleanest part of the mill. You could wear ordinary clothes to work in newsprint.

"Nah, fuck newsprint. They're all fairies in there. Steam plant's the only place to work. You never see a tour foreman in the steam plant. They're scared of the place." He looked at me and said. "You're in the bleach plant eh? Been down the kiln yet?"

"What kiln?" I hadn't heard anything about a kiln.

"I'm surprised they haven't put you in there," he said. "Now that's a tough job. The kiln."

I started graveyard shift two nights later and reported up to the bleach plant. "Unhh . . . you've got to go down to the kiln tomorrow," said Padur, the head bleach plant operator. "Persson's coming back from his vacation. It's his job you've been doing while he's been away, you know."

I didn't know. Communication wasn't big at the mill. But it was eerie how the business about the kiln had come up only a couple of days after I'd heard about it from Steam Plant Bill. It made me feel uneasy. If someone from the steam plant thought it was tough in the kiln then I wasn't sure I wanted to go there.

The limekiln horrified me right from the start. I stood and stared up its length. It was an enormous, sloping, cylindrical steel tube, rotating slowly as it cooked the lime and sifted it down towards the grate at the front; a great, gaping red hole, stretching up into infinity, ribbed with flame as far as I could see.

The best of the kiln operators was a mild-mannered man called Perkins. Perkins was close to retirement and he hardly ever spoke—except when he went into the control room to look at the dials at the beginning of his shift. He'd swear then horribly, half under his breath.

"Oh, for f . . .'s sake! It'll take us all f . . . ing night to sort this f . . . ing c . . . r out!" He'd stand in front of the console and scratch his bald head. "I don't know why they let these useless c . . . ing b . . . s in here when they don't f . . . ing well know what they're f . . . ing well doing."

Unfortunately I wasn't on the same shift as Perkins very often. If we were relieving Perkins' shift though, we'd usually be all right for the first couple of hours. After that my operator put his own stamp on the proceedings, and that was generally a bad thing.

Most of the time I worked with a young operator I'll call Don. Don was in love with a teacher from town. He wore his white hard hat on the back of his head, and he was constantly checking his image in the front glass of the control room, reflected in the red-white glare from the mouth of the kiln—instead of watching his dials and gauges.

Because he was in love, Don's mind wasn't always on the job, but he really didn't have a clue what he was doing in there anyway. The result was that he ran the kiln either too hot or too cold, often shifting the controls wildly from one extreme to the other in panic. Don usually created a wicked variety of problems for me to deal with on a shift. To cap it off, the tour foremen liked the warmth at the kiln in wintertime, and they'd come down several times a shift, and berate me if the place was untidy.

When Don ran the temperatures too cool the lime didn't cook properly; it balled up and manufactured huge, baking-hot boulders, which tumbled down and jammed up the mouth of the kiln. When that happened I had to lever them out onto the grate with a long steel bar, and then set about them with a sledgehammer and break them up into chunks small enough to shovel through the grate. The super-heated air at the front of the kiln would be hazy with quicklime dust, which settled on my skin, mixed with the sweat pouring down my arms and chest and face, climbed up my nostrils, and burned. My mouth would fill up with quicklime dust as I worked, and when I spat on the concrete floor the spit sizzled. 'Cool' was a relative term; the kiln burned at several thousand degrees, and the air temperature at the front end where I had to work was over a hundred and twenty degrees; the floor was hot enough sometimes to melt the soles of my boots.

With Don in charge I could be out on the kiln's hearth for hours, swinging the heavy sledge at lime boulders, broken blisters on my hands, while Don sat in the control room twiddling knobs and tapping the dials, pouring himself cups of coffee from his shiny steel thermos flask.

If things got out of hand—if too many boulders started coming down too fast, or too hard for the sledgehammer to break—then the kiln had to be shut down. The whole mill went down if that happened, and it brought every tour foreman and every executive out to the kiln.

At the end of a shift like that I'd be red-raw with stinging acid burns from the lime-dust. If things were really bad I could put on a pair of filthy coveralls for protection. But the coveralls were never cleaned, and were saturated with old quicklime. It was just too hot to wear much; too hot even to wear a hard hat or gloves, although gloves were usually a good idea because the metal tools burned your hands when you picked them up off the floor.

If the kiln was running too hot the tailings funnelled through a system of pipes, and down a chute into the back of a little dump truck. These tailings were toxic impurities from the lime cooking process, and they came down into the dump-cart as a fine dust, or as heavy sludge—depending on the degree of error Don had imparted into the process.

The dump-carts' ignition system was a lawnmower-type rope pull, but the machines were hardly ever serviced, and they were horribly difficult to start. Usually they did little more than cough and belch as you flailed away at the rope. When the mechanics were called to fix the problem they'd take an hour or more to arrive. By that time things would be well out of control. The mechanics hated working in the limekiln.

If the dust in the dump truck was livid green or red you knew it was volatile, that it could explode on you. It would react to sudden movements, like the dump-cart's sticky clutch, or the engine suddenly firing and dropping itself into gear before you could jump in the driver's seat. When Don got things very wrong the dump-cart filled up every few minutes. Then it would just blow up as soon as you tried to move it, and cover you from head to foot with toxic dust. When that happened you were supposed to dive under a nearby showerhead and pull the chain and soak yourself in ice-cold water.

"That stuff burns," said one of the tour foremen one night soon after I started there. "If it goes, you don't have time to take nuthin' off. You gotta get under that god-dammed shower right away." He shook his finger at the showerhead up among the caked pipes and wires and dust.

But the dump-cart sometimes kept right on exploding, with the back-up cart filling up rapidly as well. You just had to get on with it, and race the cart out of the building, past tanks and pipes and valves, and up a slippery wooden ramp which teetered round a massive pit full of sludge. This pit was out in the open air, and if it was raining, the raindrops detonated puffs of toxic dust from the mixture in the cart. The safety goggles dusted up so you couldn't see where you were going, so you had to take them off in case you drove the dumper off the ramp and ended up in the pit with all the stuff they'd been tipping in there for years.

My hard hat blew off into the pit on my first night, and I made the mistake of jumping down to retrieve it. I sank in the tailings up to my knees and only just managed to pull myself out again. Two days later the uppers on my new boots parted from the soles. The boots smelled terrible, so

I put them outside the back door of the cabin, thinking I'd get them repaired. Within a week they'd disappeared completely, rotted clean away by the residues from the kiln.

Over the course of the summer I received several promotions. Some were temporary, while people took holidays, but at the end of summer some of my colleagues went back to university, and I jumped a few rungs up the ladder.

One of these moves took me into digesters. The digesters were enormous pressure cookers which cooked up the wood chips, and distilled nasty cooking liquors. The digesters stood high up on the top floor of a building next to the bleach plant, beside the Kamyr, which was a kind of super-digester—a huge, computer-driven cooker with a tall stack which towered over the mill and spewed out a perpetual plume of white, evil-smelling smoke. On my shift Dixon ran the Kamyr, and Guy Manuel ran the digesters.

Dixon sat up in a glass control room like an eagle in an eyrie, pushing buttons and swivelling around in his chair, eating cookies and sandwiches from what seemed like a bottomless lunch bucket. Dixon's eyes went in opposite directions, so you were never quite sure when he shouted instructions whether he was talking to you or to someone else. His Kamyr must have taken considerable skill to run, but Dixon carried it off with an understated nonchalance, and rarely seemed to encounter problems.

Manuel was a young fellow from Duncan, with Latin looks and jet-black hair. He carried a rat-tailed comb in his back pocket that he whipped out whenever he passed a reflective surface. Women with high lacquered hair used to wait for him in glossy cars at the gate of the mill at the end of our shifts.

But Manuel was a hard worker. Eight digesters were fed from the top floor with wood chips, and a heavy lid of six-inch thick steel sat on top of every one, secured with about a dozen heavy bolts. These bolts had to be tightened with a big pneumatic torque wrench, which was unwieldy and difficult to handle. It was hot in there, but Manuel could work his way round these lids faster than anyone else, lifting and lowering the heavy machine, rivers of sweat pouring off him.

It occurred to me from time to time that the digesters would cause a lot of damage if they ever blew, if Manuel somehow didn't tighten one of the lids properly. The pressure inside them must have been immense. If any of them ever went off it would take the roof with it, maybe the whole building. I could never quite escape the thought, when I worked in there, that I was standing on top of eight great bombs.

Sometimes on graveyard shift, around three or four in the morning, I'd go out on the catwalk at the top of the bleach plant. It was quiet out there, with the islands sitting out on the black water under an amazing canopy of stars. The mill seemed then like a very primitive place, in a beautiful, primordial setting.

Early one November morning, my friend Scotty and I climbed to the top of Maple Mountain. The light was grey and dim, the air chill and damp. We reached the summit just before the sun rose over the far-off mainland mountains. Both of us had Second World War, bolt-action Lee Enfield .303 rifles. We were hunting for deer.

According to Scotty, the deer moved down to the valley at night to feed, and then climbed back up to the top of the mountain to sleep during the day. Our plan was to lie in wait for them as they came back to their sleeping places at dawn.

Sporadic shots reverberated through the woods as, all around the mountain, hunters potted at what they thought were deer. Scotty and I padded carefully through the woods. We weren't wearing luminescent hats or clothing, and we didn't want to be mistaken for game by hunters who were blazing away at anything that moved.

A little way down from the summit we came upon a thicket of flattened grass. It was a place where deer had been sleeping, probably the day before. Suddenly I heard a noise behind me, and spun round, jamming the rifle up to my shoulder. A deer jumped from a thicket and dashed across a glade about a hundred feet away. I flicked off the safety catch and fired at it, and then worked the bolt faster than I'd ever done when I was in the cadet corps at school in Scotland. Spent shells rained out of the breech, a fresh one going in the chamber every time I rammed the bolt home again. Although I was firing fast, and things were happening quickly, I registered the graceful, flowing movement of the deer as it sprinted through the clearing and into the forest.

I got off seven shots before the deer vanished. Scotty said it sounded like I was firing a machine gun. I'd never fired at a moving target before, and I was sure I'd missed.

"We'd better track it and make sure it's not wounded," said Scotty. "We've got to make sure; we can't just leave it."

We examined the far side of the clearing, and found some dots of blood on the moss. A few minutes later we found the deer lying on its side inside the woods. Its eyes were bright, but as I looked down at it they faded and went dull. One of my shots had gone right through the deer's heart, but it had run on for more than thirty yards before collapsing. I knew it hadn't suffered, but I also knew I'd never hunt again. The sight of the animal's life ebbing away drilled something right into my soul—something about waste, something elemental, quite beyond words.

The wages at the mill were good, and progression up the promotion ladder was sure and steady. But it gradually became obvious to me that some of the men had worked there too long, were afraid now to leave the security and predictability of the place. I could see that the mill could easily turn into a graveyard of hopes and aspirations, and I began to feel a powerful need to leave. In the spring of my second year in Canada I handed in my notice.

That second summer, I took a job as a carpenter's helper in Maple Bay. I'd decided to go to university in the autumn, and I was trying to save money. But the carpentry job didn't pay much, and it was hard to pay the bills and eat as well. Once in a while on warm nights a group of us would go down to the foreshore and collect mussels and oysters from the rocks, and cook them on a shovel over a fire on the beach. Sometimes we'd jig for codfish off the dock, or sail over to Octopus Point and build a beach fire, roast wieners and play songs on our guitars.

New people came to live in Maple Bay, and some of them took over a derelict cabin in the woods above the village. My friend Tom, who had spent the previous summer staying in my cabin while he worked at the mill, came back at the end of the university year and moved in with the squatters up on the hill.

Something indefinable and unknown crept into that sunny, perfect place, like a tiny, malevolent worm, and as the months passed it seemed as if a sense of innocence was seeping slowly away. Things began to go wrong—just small, unpleasant things at first, like fights. The culmination of it came one warm evening late in summer, when the squatters held a party at their cabin on the hill. I didn't go to the party so I wasn't clear about everything that happened, but at some point Tom and young R drove off in Tom's Pacific Blue TR3 to get some supplies at the Duncan liquor store. Tom's car was a Triumph sports car, very like mine.

The first indication that something was wrong came when a friend telephoned to see if I was all right. She sounded surprised and relieved to hear my voice. "I've just seen your little blue sports car wrapped around a telephone pole on the Maple Bay Road, near St. Peter's Church," she said. "At least I thought it was yours. There was a crowd of medics and police around it."

I knew right away what must have happened, and raced off in my car to see if I could do anything to help.

The heavy telephone pole was snapped like a matchstick, with Tom's car bent around its stump like a paperclip. R had been killed instantly. He'd been catapulted out of the passenger seat and his neck was broken. He was a lovely, bright young man of nineteen, a straight 'A' student at the University of BC.

Maple Bay was devastated, and the little church was packed for the funeral service. Tom would never be the same after that. What happened that day took away his laughter, penetrated right to the core of his life.

It was time for me to leave.

Cold War on the Pacific

The torn paper tacked onto the notice board at the wharf read:

"Deckhand Wanted.
No experience necessary. 10%.
Apply *Thornton Isle*—6B."

I went down the gangway and walked along the wooden docks until I found finger 6B. I scanned the names on the boats. *Thornton Isle* was moored near the end. It was a white boat with green trim, with fish scales and blood splotches scrubbed into its woodwork. It looked tidy enough, apart from a tangle of steel lines at its stern. A man was standing inside the cabin washing dishes. The sun was shining.

"Hello?" I knocked on the side of the boat. The man stuck his head out of the window.

"Ja?"

"There's a notice on the board at the parking lot. It says you need a deckhand."

"Ja." He nodded, and appraised me slowly. He was a thickset, grizzled man in his mid forties. "Do you haf experience?"

"The notice said you didn't need any."

He nodded again. "No," he said mildly, "but it all-vays helps."

He invited me on board and we talked for a few minutes. I told him I was studying history at university, and looking for a summer job. His accent told me he was German or Austrian, possibly Swiss. He explained that there was no guaranteed wage; the deckhand was paid ten per cent of the money from the catch. If there were lots of fish the deckhand made plenty of money. If there were no fish he didn't. The boat paid for the food, and supplied the gear.

"You can haf ze zjob," he said. "I vill teach you how to do it." He explained that Thornton Isle was a troller, a line fishing boat. The deckhand stood in a well at the back of the boat when it was fishing, working the lines, pulling in the catch. It was the deckhand's job to gut and clean the fish as they were caught, but he said that he would ice them each night himself, because that had to be done properly or the catch would spoil.

It would also be my job, he said, to cook. If we were busy catching fish, he'd take care of lunch, but breakfast and supper were mine. He stood up and reached out a big hand and told me his name was Fred Reder. He was going off to the store to buy provisions. We'd cast off at six in the morning, he said, and told me to bring warm clothes.

I got to know Fred quite well over the next couple of months. It's inevitable in a thirty-five foot boat with two people on board. You live in each other's pockets. He was German, and as I got to know him I found out what he'd done in the war. I learned as well that there were some subjects it was best not to bring up with Fred. But I came to like him. There was something solid and true about him. It became impossible to believe that a few years ago he might have been trying to kill my father, or my mother.

That first morning we didn't leave until seven-thirty because Fred had to buy fresh ice, and the ice plant wasn't open at six. He packed our food in the hold with the ice, and started up the diesel engine. We motored slowly out of Victoria's harbour, past the derelict gun emplacements at Macauley Point, and into the Straits. It was a bright May morning and the mountains on the American side were so sharp and clear they looked as if they were within spitting distance.

We sailed as far as Port Renfrew and anchored at sunset in the inlet, sheltered from any Pacific squalls that might blow up. The next day we headed into deepening swells all the way to Ucluelet, and bought fresh bait at the dock. Then we left the little west coast harbour for the big bank, forty miles offshore.

Out there just beyond the horizon the troller fleet was tracking endlessly back and forth. There must have been at least fifty boats, stretching as far as I could see. The Larousse bank was a favourite fishing ground because it was rich in feed for the salmon. The water was about forty fathoms deep, a good depth for the big springs. Fred told me there

188

were coral heads and weedy growth down on the bottom, and a host of small beings for the springs to fatten themselves up on.

Trollers can target specific species of fish, unlike the less discriminating net fishery. Each boat trails tackle from a multitude of leaders, which come off three main lines on each side, held out from the boat by two long poles. The tip line falls from the end of each pole and its leaders are held up at the surface by a styrofoam float. The mid line drops down ten or twenty fathoms. The heavy-weighted deep line is baited to catch fish near the bottom. With all that equipment in the water it's important to avoid making sharp turns. It's easy to get the lines tangled up, and wreck thousands of dollars worth of gear.

I was busy in the back of the boat when we were fishing. Whenever a fish struck the bait, a little bell attached to a spring at the top of one of the six main lines would tinkle happily. The whole line had to be winched in when that happened, and each of the leaders disconnected until I came to the one with the fish on it. I brought that line in carefully until I could stick the fish with the gaff, and haul it on board the boat. If it was a big fish which might fight its way off the leader-hook, then I'd bang it hard between the eyes with the back of the gaff, and then spike it through the head with the big hook. You didn't want to put that nasty gaff hook through the meat though, because the buyers wouldn't pay so much for it.

Fred always turned in his seat at the wheel to watch when he heard one of the little bells tinkle. Once or twice, before I got the hang of it, I knocked a fish off the hook when I clubbed it. Fred would groan when he saw a big smiley swimming away. When I asked him why they were called

smileys he grinned, and said that the fishermen called anything over twenty pounds a smiley, because at two to three
dollars a pound these big fish represented a good payday.
"They make you smile when you catch one," he said.

A couple of years later I saw an altogether different at-
titude towards these big fish when I spent a summer fishing
down the Oregon coast. The Americans didn't mess about
at all when they had a fifty or eighty-dollar fish on the line.
They'd bring their smileys (which they called splitters) alongside the boat, take out a twenty-two pistol, and shoot them
in the head. No risk, no sport; this was business.

In the time Fred and I fished out on the Larousse bank
I became used to the daily confrontations between the Canadian boats and the Russian draggers that worked out there.
These big steel Russian ships would hang around the edges
of the bank in the morning, watching the trollers at work,
eyeing us much as the Canadian fishermen watched out for
the gulls. We knew there were usually herring schools where
the gulls were flocking, and we'd head for them knowing
that salmon would be feeding on the herring from below.

The Russians would watch us for a while, then drop
their nets and plough right through the middle of the Canadian fleet. Their nets were huge, and reinforced with steel.
They hung out on big metal booms behind the trawlers,
and fell right down to the bottom and tore up all the feed
and stripped away the coral heads. When the Russians came
through the troller fleet the Canadian boats had to scatter
or be run over, or lose their gear. The Russians didn't seem
to care. There was nothing to be done about it, for in those
days the Larousse bank lay in international waters. Canada's
sovereignty only reached twelve miles out to sea. It wasn't

until the late 1970's that a two hundred mile limit was established, out to the edge of the continental shelf.

Every day we listened to confrontations on the radio. A hapless troller would be sitting in the path of an advancing Russian. The other Canadian fishermen would get on the radio and exhort their mate to stand fast.

"Don't move Charlie. You make him change his course . . ."

"Go on Charlie! You were there first. You stay where you are. Don't let the bastard make you move!"

"I'm not moving! By Christ I'm not moving! He's gonna have to go around me . . ."

"It's our goddam ocean. Jeesus! Them bastards should go fish in their own sea . . ."

"Stand up to him Charlie! Don't let them bloody Rooskies push you around."

"My lines! My goddam lines! The bastard's made me run over my f . . . ing lines. They're all f . . . ing tangled to hell . . . aaaw . . . shit!"

Time and again we'd watch a big, black, steel-hulled Russian trawler bear down on a tiny, wooden Canadian boat. Not to move was suicide. It was never a good idea to rely on any sentiments of decency or caution from the Russians.

"Christ! Next time I'm out here I'm bringing a cannon. I know a guy in Port Alberni's got one I can put up on the bow . . ."

"I've got a shotgun here. Any of them bastards comes anywhere near me, so help me I'll let him have it . . ."

We could see him through the binoculars, standing in the door of his wheelhouse, waving his arm in the air, the shotgun clutched in his fist—a popgun against an elephant. They were brave words but useless.

An anguished cry came over the radio. It was Charlie.

"The bastard . . . he's taken away my gear. The f . . . ing bastard. That's it! If I get close enough to one of those f . . . ing c . . . suckers on shore I'll f . . . ing kill him."

But there was nothing we could do. The Russians were never allowed onto our shore. Their trawlers unloaded their catches out at sea every night onto massive factory ships, which cleaned and processed the fish, and weeks later unloaded cargos of tinned salmon at Vladivostock or Nachodka, or wherever they came from. Once they were emptied the trawlers were ready to fish again until they were full. They were always out there, fishing to no limits, constrained only by how long their crews could last on the high seas without a break.

There were women on board these factory ships, we were told. They did the fish-processing work and provided unspecified services for the men.

"Some of the women," said one of the fishermen darkly in the bar at the Maquinna Hotel in Tofino one night, "are in charge of the men." He glared round the table to make sure there was no dissent. "Sure they are. They're political commissars. If the men don't do exactly what they tell 'em to do they get sent to prison camps."

"Nah . . . surely not," said one of the others uncertainly; not knowing enough to take a strong position, wanting to know more. He edged awkwardly around his question. "You don't mean they get to . . . you know . . . "

All eyes swivelled round to stare at him. He shifted in his seat.

"You know . . . get to order 'em . . . order 'em to screw 'em."

"What d'ya mean Art? Ya mean them wimmen got that much control in them ships?"

"They're commies," said the first one. "It's all the same to them. They got no moral code. They get to do what they want."

When one of the big factory ships filled up with fish, another one replaced it. It was the same with the Russian trawlers. When one left, another one took its place. You could tell when you went through an area they'd been in. The lines would go slack for an hour or more, as if a giant vacuum cleaner had passed by. Not a living thing was left in that part of the sea.

Fred and I sat out there one summer night, lifting and falling gently on the big swells. We'd packed away our gear, and fried up a spicy meal of fresh salmon fillets and fried potatoes and onions. Fresh salmon cooked in butter as soon as it's caught has no equal. It can't compare with a fish even an hour old, never mind something which has sat packaged in a store or on a fishmonger's slab. There's nothing like it. It's as different as biscuits are to bilge water.

The sun had just gone down and we'd opened the hatches to air out the boat. The dishes were done and we were waiting for the ten o'clock weather forecast to come on the radio before crawling into our sleeping bags. We went to bed with the sun out there, and got up with it too, just after four. The Russian boats were still fishing, tracking back and forth across our horizon, black against the red, western sky like patrolling Roman centurions. With their radar and echo sounders they could keep going all night.

In the opposite direction we could see the mountains on Vancouver Island, fading away now as darkness crept over the land from the east. It seemed wrong that these big ships could come here from the other side of the world and strip our fishery bare, within sight of land. It wasn't just theft; it was more like rape.

Fred began to talk to me about the war. Earlier that day we'd had an argument about concentration camps. Fred said he didn't believe they'd existed. "I vould haf known about zem if they had," he insisted.

"You must have seen the films," I countered. "You can't deny the films—you must have seen them."

"I only saw zem after the var. Zhey ver made by the people who von the var."

I told him I'd known people in Scotland when I was growing up who'd seen the camps and that I believed them. But it wasn't a good thing to talk with him about, and we let the subject go.

It was amazing to me then that I could be sitting out on the Pacific Ocean, sharing supper with someone who'd fought in the war on the other side, a fellow Canadian now. In Edinburgh, when I was growing up, our next-door neighbours were Scots; I knew where they came from; more or less how they thought, what they believed. It was clear which side they'd fought on in the war. The people they'd fought against were 'over there', across the sea. Abroad. They lived in foreign countries, spoke different languages. They didn't live in our cities and walk our streets.

The war was all around me when I was growing up in Scotland, even though it had been over for years. Some of my school friends didn't have fathers—they'd been killed in the fighting. George Bain's dad was shot down right at the end of his tour of flying operations, on his last trip, a month before George was born. One of my uncles had been in a

Japanese prison camp; another in photo reconnaissance; a third at the great naval battle of the River Plate. A picture of my dad in his RAF uniform sat on the mantelpiece in my bedroom. In the streets we'd encounter men with missing arms, or on crutches and with one leg—with the empty trouser leg pinned up behind them—or perhaps in a wheelchair, with no legs at all. They were as common a sight as a game of football in the park.

But here in Canada my next-door neighbour could be Japanese or German, or Chinese or Italian. No matter what they'd done in the past they were all Canadians now—as much as I was. I'd worked at the pulp mill with a Japanese student who lived in the same village as I did. I had no idea what his parents had done in the war. One of my friends had a German father. In this country it didn't seem to matter. People's names never told you which side they'd been on either, because people of all nationalities had fought for Canada and the Commonwealth. To me it was one of the finest things about Canada then; that the people themselves made up the country in a way that seemed to transcend the tight European politics which had led over the centuries to so many wars.

Fred had been a pilot in the Luftwaffe. He'd flown twin-engined, Messerschmitt 110 night fighters. He didn't know how many aeroplanes he'd shot down, he said; he didn't keep track of these things like some of the other pilots did. He told me proudly that he had a metal plate in his head, put there by a British surgeon after he was shot down one night on an intruder operation over Bradford. He pointed to a white scar that ran from the top of his forehead up under his hairline, and told me that the English doctor who eventually patched him up said that a piece of shrapnel had cut open his head.

Fred thought that he must have been shot down by anti-aircraft fire. When his night-fighter caught fire he managed to get out of it, and he came down to earth by parachute. He landed in the grounds of a country house which belonged to the Duchess of Bradford. The Duchess was having a party at the time, and the guests ran out and carried Fred off to the house, where they sat him down, plied him with brandy, and bandaged him up. By the time the Home Guard came to take him away he wasn't feeling any pain at all.

There was a bit more to his story than that. Fred told me later he thought the Duchess became quite infatuated with him—this blond, bloodied warrior who dropped into her garden from the sky. He said she tried to come and see him in the prison camp but the authorities wouldn't allow it.

We left the bank soon after that, with the Russians still patrolling back and forth along the line of the horizon. We sailed into Barkley Sound and refuelled at Bamfield, a little west coast community with a narrow inlet for a main street. After trying our luck off Pachena we anchored one starry night in a bay just off the beach. The next day we followed the coast down to the waterfall at Cloo-oos, near the mouth of the Straits, where the fishing was supposed to be good. But there were no fish there, and we moved on before nightfall. This stretch of the coast is known as the 'Graveyard of the Pacific.' It's far too open and unpredictable for safe anchoring. We moved on south, and anchored in San Juan inlet just before dark.

There was a fight that night in the pub at Port Renfrew. Although I wasn't involved in it, Fred saved me from being brained by a chair. He reached out and closed one of his massive ham-like hands round the neck of one of the fighters and moved him firmly off to one side. The guy dropped the chair, and fell over, then got up and took a long look at Fred before deciding to stay out of his way. After all that time at sea with him I was glad Fred was on my side.

Sunshine Valley

It's late summer and warm in the valleys, but the air is becoming crisp as the old Chevy climbs into the mountains. It's a '59 Chev with wide gull wings at the back, and big, garish tail lights like soup plates, and it doesn't like the long inclines.

I'm heading up the Trans Canada Highway to a job at Sunshine Valley, about twenty miles west of Banff. It's a construction job and it pays well. Sunshine is one of the top ski areas in the Canadian Rockies, and I've been hired to help build a new lift in time for the coming season.

The car coughs and heaves its way up between wooded mountainsides towards the resort. It's a big car, lemon yellow, and wide enough for me to sleep along its bench seats. This saves money with motels and lodgings, although it has occurred to me that the car's voracious thirst for gasoline must offset these economies.

Sunshine Valley sits on the Alberta-British Columbia border, and the road deteriorates as it climbs, until it's little more than a cart track. Snow falls at Sunshine even in summer, and the banks of dirt-grey hard-pack at the side of the trail grow higher as I climb deeper into the mountains. I decide to leave the Chev in a clearing at the bottom of the last steep pitch. Miraculously, a sturdy yellow mountain bus turns up to collect me, and carries me up the long hill to the resort.

Sunshine Village consists of two lodges. One of them is undergoing a face-lift. Like most ski resorts in summertime, the area looks dingy and down-at-heel without the softening effects of fresh snow. All around the village the mountains rise up into a deep blue sky. This alpine valley sits at seven thousand feet, and the air is much thinner than it is down in Banff; something I notice right away when I climb up stairs.

I'm given a room, and directions to the canteen. There's hardly anyone around, and the people I meet don't speak much. Mountain people are taciturn anyway, and wary of strangers, so this doesn't surprise me.

My room is small and dark, and faces onto a bare hillside. In the month that I'm here, the sun never comes through the window. The room has a bed and a chair, and a small chest-of-drawers, nothing more. Meal times are posted on a sheet of paper tacked on the back of the door.

A dozen of us are working up here on the new lift, and the daily procedure is straightforward. The day begins with someone beating a metal triangle at six-thirty. We get up and shower, and walk over for breakfast in the canteen.

199

This is always a hearty meal, with limitless quantities of eggs and bacon, toast, hash browns and coffee, and sometimes thick, Alberta steaks. The company feeds us well, in order to insulate us against the uncertainties of weather and altitude. Before we go out, we make lunch from hams and roasts, lettuces and salad pieces. The company supplies us with coffee flasks and juice containers. Signs around the canteen warn us that altitude saps the body of fluids; that it's important to keep ourselves well hydrated.

By eight we're ready to go. We load up with picks, shovels and backpacks, and start the hike up the mountain. I'm assigned to the top station, right at the summit of Mount Brewster. The summit lies just over nine thousand feet above sea level. From the lodge it's a climb of two thousand feet— two thousand feet, first thing in the morning, all the way to the very top before starting work. Three of us set off together. We're all about the same age. Jeff comes from Calgary, Greg from Banff. They're tough Canadian boys, resourceful and uncomplaining. Greg has taken a year out of university, but Jeff left school after grade ten. I learn a lot from them in a short time. It stands me in good stead sooner than I might have thought.

The climb is steep, and each of us has a heavy, awkward load to carry, so we don't talk much. The valley falls away below us, and the village and its brown chalets shrink into the scenery. As we climb higher, the Canadian Rockies open out in magnificent scales of light and shade, sharp and pale with morning sunlight. They look untouched, as if we're the first people ever to see them.

Half way up the mountain we pass the crumpled wreck of a helicopter, a heap of twisted blue and white metal, its perspex windscreen shattered into tiny, shiny fragments. It's

200

hard to see how anyone could have come out of the accident alive. Two of the work crew quit right away when it happened. That's how I got the job. There were vacancies.

Greg and Jeff each stop off at separate tower foundations as we make our way up the mountain. I'm the last, and I climb the final pitches by myself, to the sound of my own rough breathing. By the time I reach the top I'm ready for a rest and a cup of coffee. It's a breathtakingly clear morning, with the view spread out below my feet as far as I can see, in every direction.

Far across the valley in front of me stand the massive walls of the Monarch, its sheer, grey sides cold and menacing, and topped with a thick, flat cap of snow. I feel like an eagle floating on the sky. Twenty miles to the east, Mount Assiniboine rises up like a jagged tooth. Assiniboine is Canada's Matterhorn, an isolated pinnacle of rock, elegant and picturesque, and dangerous. The valley below me is studded with tiny blue lakes. These high valleys are wild moorlands, rarely travelled by people, covered in winter with a thick snow-pack. They're home to wild animals; deer live up here, and bear, and sometimes, wolves. On this early summer morning the heaths absorb the light in a gentle, purple haze, which suggests abundant berries and other nourishing foods.

Far down the mountain the replacement helicopter starts up, its long turbine whine like a bitter arctic wind. The chopper will deliver big buckets of slurry cement up the mountainside for us to dump into the tower foundations. But first, it's my job to dig a deep, wide hole with a pick and shovel in the dirt and shale of the summit, and then lace its inside with reinforcing metal rods. This will be the foundation for the top lift tower on the mountain. When the hole is ready I'll have to stand on its edge under the hovering helicopter, steady the bucket, and pull a lever to dump the concrete.

The helicopter accident happened at the steepest pitch on the mountainside. Up here in the mountains, the wind always blows uphill. The pilot must face the chopper into the wind when he's hovering, so he can keep everything as stable as possible while the man on the ground empties the cement into the hole. The ground man can easily be injured by the heavy bucket swinging about at the end of its steel line twenty feet below the helicopter, or an expensive load can be wasted if it misses the hole. It's tricky flying and it takes a lot of skill. It also takes a steady nerve from the man on the ground.

Two days ago the pilot flew up from Sunshine Village with the bucket underneath, and slowly let down over the tower-foundation hole, three towers down from the top. He turned the helicopter gingerly around to face into the wind, but the slope was very steep there, and the tail rotor hit the hillside and splintered and spun off. This instantly destroyed the helicopter's lateral stability. The main rotor spun the whole contraption out of control, and it crashed down the mountainside like a giant eggbeater, smashing itself to bits.

The pilot was lucky to get out of it alive. They sent a Medevac chopper up from the hospital in Banff, and took him away with many broken bones and a badly cut up face. Greg told me they put a hundred and six stitches in the pilot's face alone. The guy guiding the bucket on the ground quit on the spot.

It doesn't bear thinking about, and neither does the sheer three thousand-foot drop over the back, less than ten feet from where I'm working. I swing away grimly, loosening the rock with the pick and tossing it off to one side with the shovel. It's unbelievably hard work in the thin air at this altitude. At the top of Mt. Brewster I'm sitting right on the Alberta-British Columbia border, nine thousand feet above sea level.

A new man joins our crew. They put him to work on the new lift line, but down near the bottom of the mountain. He wears an American university fraternity jacket with a big letter 'O' stitched on its chest. The new fellow claims he's at the University of Oregon and talks a big line. At dinner and breakfast he regales us with his exploits on the college track team, how he's made the varsity basketball team, smashed defensemen into the ground in football games. He has the answer to every question on any subject. Any new piece of information that's offered—he knew it all along. Soon, no one wants to work with him. The others avoid him in the evenings. He already has his nickname. It comes from the letter on his jacket. We call him Zero.

It's amazing how your appetite expands in the mountain air. After work each of us can eat several steaks—with eggs, bacon and beans—and wash it all down with quarts of coffee. One warm evening we discover that the trail horses are back, corralled a hundred yards away from our billets. Greg tells me that the trail ride company wants us to exercise them during the week, so they won't go soft and out of shape waiting for the next group of tourists on the weekend.

In the evenings, after supper, we tack up the horses and take them out. Mine is a big roan called Blue, and he carries me up into one of the high canyons round the back of Mt. Brewster. This is wild country, with small scrub trees, high meadows and tiny lakes. Greg knows it well, and we take our time, and savour the warm summer air of the mountains. The horses stop periodically to munch on the nourishing grasses. High up the canyon under Mt. Brewster's northern face, Blue refuses to go on. He tosses his head and whinnies, but he won't budge.

Greg sniffs at the wind. "Something's spooked him," he mutters. "Might be a cat." There are cougar up here, and bears. Bears have a strong, musky smell; I can't smell anything at all. "The horses know," says Greg. We turn back.

The next day I finish digging the main part of my hole on top of the mountain. It's ready for its first dump of concrete. It will take several buckets. Jeff climbs up from his workplace five hundred feet below. It takes three people to work a dump, two on the ground and one in the air. Jeff stands off to one side to guide the pilot with hand signals. Up or down, to one side or the other. I'll stand underneath the chopper, on the rim of the hole I've dug, and steady the bucket and pull the lever to drop the cement.

The helicopter winds up from the valley, and swings far out over the heath and the tarns, the bucket out almost to the horizontal at the end of its line as the chopper banks to make the turn up towards the top of the mountain. The clatter of the blades fills the air. Only turbines can work effectively at this altitude.

The helicopter lets down slowly over the summit, until the bucket is hanging a few feet above my head. Jeff is giving hand signals, standing off to one side so that the pilot can see him. Down a little, left, left, down a bit more. The pilot's skill is amazing. His trust in Jeff is even more astonishing. As far as I know Jeff has never done this before, has never had any training for this kind of air traffic control.

The bucket sways one way and swings back. I try to steady it, but it weighs several tons, and brushes me aside like a fly, almost toppling me into the hole. This is the most dangerous part of the whole procedure, and it takes great concentration. If the chopper gets into trouble the pilot will instantly hit an emergency button in the cockpit, and drop the bucket and line. Anyone underneath it will be crushed. I can imagine the pilot's hand hovering over the button as he waits for me to dump the cement out of the bucket.

I reach for the lever at the side of the bucket and give it a heave. The trap opens and spews a couple of tons of wet cement into the hole. Some of it splashes over the rim. Jeff waves the chopper off and it shoots up like an express elevator, and swings off down the mountain.

"Good dump," says Jeff laconically. I stare down at my boots. They're covered in wet cement. "Not bad for a first attempt."

It's easy to see, standing under that enormous bucket, how the man on the ground could be knocked flying in a split second of bad judgement. It's easy to see too, that it must be nerve-wracking further down the mountain, where the slope is so steep that the pilot has to manoeuvre with his tail rotor only a foot or two from the hillside.

I spend the afternoon welding re-bar together, and jamming rods into the wet slurry. The welding mask is cumbersome, so I take it off in order to see better. This is a stupid thing to do, but I've never done any arc welding before, and no one has taught me anything about it.

It's some time before I realise that the day has darkened and the wind has come up. On the far side of the valley, a massive black cloud has swallowed up the Monarch. The cloud flickers with bright yellow flashes, which light it up from the inside. Long, evil-looking streamers trail from its base, whipping around in vortices created by the crashing together of warm and freezing air currents. The cloud is

205

heading straight towards me, gliding inexorably across the high valley towards Mt. Brewster, rumbling and crackling, jumping with electricity, as if it's alive. It's the most violent storm I've ever seen.

For the first time I realise just how much metallic junk has accumulated up here on top of the mountain. The summit is strewn with pieces of re-bar, lengths of girder and various other metal components for building the lift tower. It looks as if the storm cloud will hit Mt. Brewster about a thousand feet below where I'm working, and envelop me completely within the next few minutes. When it does, I'll be standing in the middle of a vicious electrical storm, astride the highest point for miles, surrounded by pieces of steel and iron, all of them magnets for lightning bolts.

There doesn't seem to be much I can do about it. It's not a good idea to try and make my way down the mountain with a storm like this only minutes away. Dangerous cliffs and drop-offs, some of them hundreds of feet high, lie waiting for the unwary traveller. It wouldn't be difficult to fall from one of these. Visibility inside the cloud will be very poor.

The hole I've dug for the lift-tower foundation is not completely filled with wet cement, and I can just squeeze onto a small ledge inside it. A sheet of plywood is lying nearby, and a small square of tarpaulin. I build myself a tiny shelter in a hurried two minutes, and hop into the hole.

The cloud blots out the daylight, and envelops the whole mountain seconds later. A huge flash lights up my hole. An enormous crash goes off simultaneously, like a bomb, followed by another crash and another; then more flashes. The noise is tremendous. Through a space where the plywood rests on the stones at the edge of my hole I can see lightning dancing all over the summit. The electric light seems to ricochet from one piece of metal to another. My hair stands on end from the electricity. It's an awe-inspiring demonstration of the power of nature and it nearly frightens the life out of me.

The storm lasts about fifteen minutes, although it seems like hours. The storm cloud eventually drifts on to the next mountain, crashing and banging its way across the valley. The sun comes out to glaze the rain-slicked rocks and polish the metal. I'm exhausted.

That night my eyes begin to sting. The pain increases until it's almost unbearable, as if someone has tossed ground glass under my eyelids. Nothing can relieve the agony of it. This is the price I'm paying for welding without protective goggles, but I don't realise this until late the next day when someone takes me down to Banff to see the doctor. He applies some drops, which fix up my eyes in minutes. It's a hard lesson to learn, but it's nothing beside the awesome power of the elements that I saw a few hours ago. I'm lucky to be around to feel pain at all.

By the time I leave the doctor's surgery it's dusk. I've decided to stay the night with friends who live at the edge of town, and I set off to walk to their house. I take a road up the steep side of Tunnel Mountain, high above the valley, past suburban houses. A man is putting his garbage out on the sidewalk as I turn a corner. It occurs to me that he's making quite a job of it, banging the bucket about and making a lot of noise. He knocks the lid off, and it clatters onto the road. Then he sticks his head in the bucket as if he's dropped something inside. It's hard in the gathering dark to see exactly what he's doing, but his behaviour seems very odd. He's a big man too, and as I draw closer to him I'm almost floored by an overpowering body odour. In the same second I realise that it's not a man at all, but a big, hungry bear, rummaging for food.

I don't know whether to turn and run, or whether that will startle the bear and make it aggressive. I don't know either if it's a grizzly or a brown bear, or a black one. Each type has different characteristics, and presents varying degrees of danger. I have only a second or two to make a decision, for to stop this close to the bear will be asking for trouble. I cross the street, holding a steady pace, fighting the urge to run. The bear pays no attention to me at all. When I'm past him, I quicken my pace. Twenty yards down the road I'm running like hell.

King of the Hill

I'm surprised to find the little cabin still standing, where I spent the winter in 1971. No one seems to be living here at the moment, but whoever owns it now has fixed it up in pretty pastel paintwork, with shades of pasty grey for the doors and window frames. The front step has been repaired, and the cabin has a new roof. The comfortable grumble of the fast-flowing Zigzag River draws me round to the rear, where I discover a new sundeck, and trees cut back to give the place some air, and let in the sun. I stand and gaze at the river as it rollicks past the old cabin's back door, and think for a moment of its origins among the high, snow-laden crevasses under the summit of Mount Hood.

I've come to this place much as I did in 1971, by following US 26 east from Portland, up the south bank of the great Columbia River. On this side of the mountains the highway criss-crosses the historic Barlow Trail, the old wagon route which brought settlers west from Independence, Missouri, through the Rockies and across the Cascade range to Oregon's fertile Willamette Valley. It's an area rich with American folklore—full of the lusty, gutsy energy that overcame a hostile landscape, and months of virtually insurmountable deprivations—and yet somehow in American legend managed to ally itself with the idea of families and children. When I first came here though, I knew hardly anything about the place.

I drove through the village of Rhododendron, deep in the wooded foothills of the Cascade Mountains on Oregon's wet, west side. My little British sports car was almost out of gas and there were less than twenty dollars left in my pocket. It was Canadian money too, not American greenbacks. Americans wouldn't accept the funny-coloured Canadian dollars, and the banks were closed. It was six o'clock on the evening of New Year's Day, and it was already dark. Looking for Road 35, I only had the vaguest idea of where I was going.

The forest began to hem the road in as it climbed deeper into the Cascades, and snow banks rose higher and higher on each side. Tough as it was, my little Triumph TR4, with its soft-top canvas roof wasn't the sort of vehicle for these conditions, and its old, worn tires were hardly fitted for winter. When I eventually found it, Road 35 was impassable, its entrance blocked by snow from passing snowploughs. I squeezed the Triumph into a tiny alcove in the snowbank alongside the deserted highway, and hauled my bag out of the space behind the seats. I climbed out and headed into the woods, following a winding gap through the trees, fastening my jacket against the biting cold. I hoped it was the track of the invisible Road 35, but right from the start I was breaking trail, wading through deep snow up to my thighs, my city shoes already filled with the stuff, my legs growing numb. There was no sign of any habitation, nothing to indicate people.

I was more than half a mile into the forest before I came to a cabin, and wondered in the gathering dark whether I was anywhere near the target of the hazy directions I'd been given by my cousin. The cabin looked utterly deserted—a wreck, with paint peeling from its walls, and thick moss growing over rotting roof shakes under a lip of snow. One side of the front step had broken off, and the other looked as if it would collapse at the next footfall. Round the back a broken, weatherworn deck leaned drunkenly out towards a rushing, narrow river, bright with the kind of glacial meltwater I'd seen the previous summer in the Rockies. The place was dark and deserted, and looked as if no one had lived there for months.

The cabin was owned by a man in Portland who just wanted someone to live in it through the winter, and keep the pipes from freezing. Somehow my New Zealand cousin John had latched onto it, and he'd been living there since autumn. John was a good skier who had been on the fringes of the New Zealand Olympic team. He'd landed himself a short-term job running a ski school on Mt. Hood, and I'd come down here to join him because I couldn't get any work up north—despite my brand new university degree.

I circle the cabin again and walk back through the trees to the dirt road. I lived here for nearly seven months. It's funny to think it was my home once. Seven months is a long time.

211

When I lived here none of my friends up north, or my family in Scotland, knew where I'd gone.

There was no central heating in the tumbledown shack, no heating of any kind, except for a big river-stone fireplace in the main room. A couple of weeks after I moved in we managed to scrounge a truckload of teak ends from a carpenter down in Wemme. The teak blocks burned with a tremendous heat and left hardly any ash. But we didn't have enough money to buy any more wood, so the teak had to last. It was a small cabin and the heat didn't have far to go once the fire was lit, but the fire never stayed on all night, and the floor was usually furred with frost in the mornings. The interior walls were made out of hardboard, which bulged and warped in the damp cold.

Road 35 was choked with drifts until the end of March that year, and I had to hike in and out, half a mile at each end of the day, until the snow melted. I walk back up the road, trying to remember how familiar it must once have been—but now the track has twists and turns I can't recall.

"Got you a job," said John that night, when he eventually turned up. "Ski Instructor up at Multorpor." I knew that Multorpor was one of the main ski areas on the mountain, up on the ridge, near the crest of the Barlow Pass.

I pointed out to him that I couldn't ski.

"That doesn't matter. I'll work with you," he said cheerfully. "We'll do dry-land training every night, and we can ski every day. You'll pick it up quickly enough."

"No gear either," I went on, "I don't have any equipment."

"No problem. I'll speak to the Garcia rep on the weekend. He supplies all the instructors with equipment. He'll get you skis, bindings and poles. I ordered some new boots yesterday, so you can have my old ones when the new ones come."

Right away we started out on a compressed training programme. Night after night John subjected me to bone-stretching contortions in front of the fire in the cabin on Road 35.

"Technique!" he said. "You can learn it just as well in here as you can on the hill."

We stuck to it night after night, although most of the time I didn't know what John was talking about. "Drive your knees into the hill, so the inside edges carve into the slope," he said. "That'll stop you sliding downhill . . ." and then "upper body out . . . face it out! Down the hill. That's right! Knees into the hill, upper body out . . . Anticipation!" and on and on like that, bending me like a pretzel.

One evening a pair of shiny new red and white Kneissl skis were delivered to the cabin, fitted with top-of-the-line Marker bindings. Two Kastle ski poles stood beside them. The local ski rep had sent them along for me to use, just as John had said he would. The next day John's new Lange boots arrived at the door in a box. Lange's were reckoned to be the best boots on the market. John opened the box and tried on the boots, and handed me his old ones, which were not even a year old. He tossed me a smart ski jacket. "It's last year's model," he said, as if that made it all right for me to parade around in such a fancy outfit.

"I can't wear this stuff," I told him. "It's ridiculous! It'll be obvious to anyone up there that I haven't got a clue how to ski."

"Nonsense," said John. "You've got nothing to worry about. You'll be right as rain in a few days. King of the hill! You wait and see."

After a week of dry land training he decided that I was ready for a public appearance. Besides, the clamour was rising up the mountain for the hot skier from Scotland to turn up.

Ten minutes after we entered the lodge at Multorpor I found out that I'd been skiing for years—a member of the elite Dundee Ski Club in Scotland.

"I hear it's one of the oldest clubs in the world," said a healthy-looking girl with a US Ski Instructors Association badge on her sweater.

John coughed and avoided my eye.

"Tell me," asked one of the older American instructors reverently, "Is the Dundee Ski Club really the same sort of thing to skiing as the Royal and Ancient Society is to golf?"

Rubbery at the knees, I nodded at them speechlessly.

My accent was unmistakably Scots, so that part of it was all right. It was even true that I'd skied once or twice when I was a boy at Ben Lawers and Coire Cas, two of the pioneer ski areas in Scotland. The ski tow at Coire Cas then was a knotted rope, powered by the rusting remains of an amphibious WWII landing craft called a Weasel. At Ben Lawers you hiked up the mountain and skied down, and repeated the process until you were too exhausted to do it any more. It was a far cry from the sleek Mueller lifts which whisked people up the slopes of Mt. Hood.

A small crowd had gathered outside the Lodge at Multorpor to watch my debut, and there was nothing I could do about it. John saw what was in the wind and quietly departed for the ski lift. Carefully I stepped into the brand new Kneissl skis, and they immediately took off on their own as if they were greased. I reared up on one leg like a circus acrobat and then fell down.

John miraculously re-appeared, helped me to the edge of a gentle incline and gave me a push. I shot off down the hill in a kind of jack-knifed, boxer's crouch, unable to deviate to the right or left. When I came to a stop on the up-slope, I slid backwards down the hill and fell over again. I picked myself up and found the audience had evaporated.

We decided that it was better to keep me away from the public gaze for a while, but I kept working at my technique in a quiet corner of the ski area. I skied all day, and continued under the floodlights every night. Each night before bed John and I did twenty minutes of dry land work. I skied and skied—using the free lift pass I'd been given on the strength of John's line.

Three days after my first effort at Multorpor my cousin decided I was ready for the Upper Bowl. He was impatient to get me working. He took me higher and higher on successive lifts, until we reached the crest of a knife-like ridge. When I picked myself up at the foot of the exit ramp I was horrified to find that we had to inch along a narrow trail with a sheer drop on either side. John skated carelessly ahead, calling over his shoulder for me to follow. A few minutes later I was staring down a vertical chute which was stacked with huge, slab-sided moguls. The Upper Bowl was a place strictly for experts.

John disappeared over the edge with a cheery, "Follow me!"

I looked wildly about for another route, but there was no other way down the mountain. I side-slipped after him, and immediately crashed. I got up and edged gingerly down the hill and crashed again, and then slid at gathering speed on my back all the way to the bottom, collecting several angry skiers in a mobile, tangled scrum.

Each day I was afraid they were going to take away my ski pass. Every night I went back to the Ski Bowl, and skied under the lights until they switched them off. It was easier at night in the soft yellow light, skiing among shadows which outlined all the bumps and dips.

One day I was ready to conduct my first elementary class. I had read the instructor's manual from cover to cover, and I planned to stay a step ahead of the pupils by reviewing the book before each class. I was never short of pupils, perhaps because I was keen, and fresh at it. At the end of February I entered a giant slalom race, and won a small bronze medal. A few days later John flew back to New Zealand, leaving me with the cabin, and a beckoning career as a ski instructor.

The road through Government Camp seems wider now. The village has grown into a mountain suburbia since I lived here, although the Ratskellar Pub still stands at its centre like a big hay barn, and the silver Trailways bus sits outside Huckleberry's Café as if it's been waiting there for passengers through all the years.

The skiers who come up here have a choice of four ski areas, all of them lying in the shadow of Mt. Hood, one of the great volcanic peaks of the Cascades. The mountain rises up more than eleven thousand feet—a full five thousand feet above the tree line—shimmering white in the sun, or glowering through mist. It's a dormant volcano, and when you climb high enough you can smell sulphur fumes up by Crater Rock.

When I lived here I sometimes spent nights up on the mountain, staying in the warm cabins of the friends I made there. These cabins were scattered along the summer woodland trails around Government Camp, nestled in winter among deep snowdrifts.

Buffy's cabin had a big airtight stove which pumped out heat. It was always cosy in there. Buffy worked as a waitress at Timberline Lodge until she got her ski instructor's ticket. She'd moved out west from Minnesota, and she took in anyone who needed a bed. A steep, icy trail led up through the forest to her cabin, over snow so deep that you had to slide down a hole to reach her back door. The back door opened into a basement where visitors stacked their skis and took off their wet clothes. A staircase led up from there to a trapdoor, which opened into Buffy's living room. You never knew who you'd find up there. A couple of bedrooms sat like bird's nests under the eaves, and there was usually soup or stew bubbling on the stove.

A strange mix of people lived up on Mt. Hood that winter, some of them permanent residents, others just passing through. Despite this transience the place had an air of stability, a sense of its own history.

Some of the permanent residents were fine skiers—like Bud Valian, who owned a small ski shop. People said Bud was the best skier there'd ever been on the mountain, but I never saw him ski. A few years before I lived on the mountain, Bud had skied down from Timberline Lodge one night, late. A local logging contractor had left a wire hawser strung across the trail. Bud skied into it and broke both his legs so badly that the doctor didn't think he'd ever walk again.

Lorita Leuthold sold lift tickets at the Multorpor Day Lodge, a lovely, dignified woman who had lost her husband on Mt. Hood. Joe Leuthold had died in the crevasse field under the summit, high up on the mountain's western flank, somewhere near the source water of the Zigzag River. Lorita never spoke of it.

Brian McEneny was a ski instructor with bad knees, who lived in an apartment above a ski shop, across the road from the pub. Brian would argue for hours about ski technique. He claimed that he didn't follow any particular technique—he simply moved his feet around and his skis went where he wanted them to go. He skied brilliantly, with almost no body movement north of his ankles. He never wore socks, he said, because it gave him a better feel for the snow.

Brian worked sometimes with the ski patrol, and he took me up on the ridges to knock off cornices, which could break off and cause avalanches. It was dangerous work, jumping up and down on the overhangs; you had to know when the cornice was about to go—know when to leap off before it collapsed.

All the ski patrol were good skiers. Some nights I went out with them at half past ten, as soon as the mountain closed down. The patrol had to make sure that no one was left on the hill; that no one was lying out there with a broken leg. They called this last run 'the sweep', and they made it after all the lights had been turned off. It was majestic to stand up on the empty mountainside, in the perfect silence of the Oregon night, and gaze up at Mt. Hood, luminescent in the moonlight. I began to understand why some people worship mountains. The skis hissed quietly on the snow as we glided along, feeling as if we were floating down from the stars.

Then there were the drifters. They came from all over the United States, some from other countries; most of them chasing dreams, or looking for adventures; some of them putting distance between themselves and past lives.

Jerry and Jamie came from the Azores—Portuguese islands, far out in the Atlantic Ocean. They both worked up at Timberline Lodge, running lift lines and driving snow cats. Anselm and Lionel came from France. I'd come from Scotland, via Canada.

Sandy was a drifter from New Hampshire who spent his summers working carnivals around Santa Rosa in California. He was thin and blond and quiet, and in winter he worked on the lifts at Timberline. There was something infinitely sad about Sandy, but I never managed to discover what it was. I think he'd been married once.

Sandy never skied and, unlike the others, he never talked about skiing. When he went to work he rode the lift up the mountain, and at the end of the day he rode it down to the Lodge, and took the Timberline taxi back down to the village. I asked him once why he never skied, and he told me that his skis had been stolen. People offered to lend him skis but Sandy always turned them down.

But one day near the end of that winter I was walking down the road from Government Camp. I'd been invited to supper with some friends who lived at the Thundermug, a small bar-hotel near the main road. I saw a figure gliding along the fringe of the woods on top of a steep bank above me, where the snow was old and drifted, and softened by advancing spring. It was lumpy, difficult snow, very difficult for most people to ski.

The figure I could see was floating in and out of the snow as if he was moving through fresh, light powder—as if he was dancing. It was Sandy, and he didn't see me; didn't see anyone else at all. He was completely at home on his borrowed orange skis, in a way I could never be, even if I skied for a hundred years.

I never again saw him on skis.

Charlie Huff knew how to fix things—a lovely, quiet man, and a fine skier. Charlie was going to go back to university one day to study mechanical engineering. Charlie was killed a year or two after I left the mountain, crushed by a lift engine which dropped on him.

Chico made leather belts, and straps and jackets and hats. He was a wild, exuberant, generous man, dark and swarthy, and he came from Colorado. He lived with Patti in a tiny cabin near Joe Engelsby's dog kennels. Eventually Chico moved up to Sundance in Idaho.

People came and went, chasing dreams or running way. It didn't matter. We lived up there in a world of our own, insulated from the business and politics of the rest of the continent, sharing what we had, borrowing what we needed. The people who lived in the Cascades were independent people, like the pioneers who'd trekked over these mountains more than a century before. Few of them asked personal questions, not because they weren't curious, but because they weren't nosy. Two years after I left, hardly any of the people who had made their homes up on Mt. Hood that winter were still there.

Most of us treated the flatlanders with disdain. The flatlanders were the people who flocked up to the mountain on weekends in designer ski wear—the glossy people from Portland and Eugene, and the towns in the Willamette Valley. They had all the right equipment—expensive boots and skis, and shiny 'wet look' clothing. Most of us just had blue jeans and hand me downs, and anything we could scrounge from the manufacturers' reps when they passed through.

But we could ski. Many of the people who lived up on the mountain were experts, and by the time John left for New Zealand at the end of February I could keep up with most of them. The flatlanders looked good, but few of them were in the same league as us on skis. We tolerated them, but we didn't mix with them very well. We were young, and arrogant with it, but we were broke too, and we didn't have much else except a misplaced pride in what we could do. And the mountain belonged to us. We felt as if we owned it.

Early in the morning, and sometimes when the sun went down, the mountain turned a rose-pink colour and seemed to float above the foothills. Whenever I went down to Portland I would look up from the busy city streets to make sure the mountain was still there, soaring high and white above the green Cascades. It gave me a warm feeling to see it, and I would hurry through whatever I was doing so I could get back to it.

It was the same for all of us; it was the way we thought, but you had to live up there to understand it. The mountain was probably the only permanent thing we had.

The Man Who Skied Down Mountains

Mt. Hood is a dormant volcano. It's a sacred mountain, steeped in legend and mythology for the Sahaptin Indians, who call it Wy'east. Just under the summit lie vents and holes called fumaroles, and sometimes the heat of the mountain hollows out big snow caves, which fill with toxic sulphur fumes and sometimes overcome climbers who explore them.

At the beginning of the twentieth century a man called Lija Coleman built a two-storey cabin on the summit of Mt. Hood. He carried the building materials up on his back, without using pack mules. When the cabin was finished he anchored it with wire cables against the winds which blow mightily up there at eleven thousand feet. Lija Coleman lived on his mountaintop during the summers, and sometimes in winter too. His cabin lasted for nearly twenty years before it blew away. The cables are still up there, anchored onto the summit rock.

When I lived on the mountain we would sometimes gather at the Thundermug, where the side road from Government Camp joins US 26. The motel was owned by the same people who ran Timberline Lodge, but it never seemed to have any paying guests. Several of the ski instructors lived there.

Anselm Baud was one of the instructors at Timberline. He had come to Oregon with another Frenchman called Lionel Wibault. The two of them had been members of the French 'B' Ski team when the French were dominating the World Cup racing circuit. Lionel had come from Morzine, near Chamonix, and he ran a racing school at Mt. Hood Meadows on the east side of the mountain. Although their English was quite good, the two Frenchmen both liked to speak in their native language. I spoke some French, and I became friends with them.

Lionel was a fast skier, a downhill racer. He often pace-set races when there were USSA competitions on the mountain. The pacesetter tested out the course, and established a time standard. Lionel was so fast that he would sometimes post the best time of the day—unusual for a forerunner on a fresh course. He even beat Jungle Jim Hunter, the Canadian world cup skier, once.

Anselm was a different type of skier from Lionel. He was fluid and quick—slalom-quick. Anselm could ski in any weather, and he was a fully qualified Alpine guide. I often skied with him, and learned much just by watching him. He negotiated every kind of terrain with a perfect grace, fusing art and athleticism in the fluent way he moved across his snowy landscapes.

He was an unassuming, gentle fellow, but Anselm's French accent was fateful to women, who were attracted to him like bees to a plot of clover. There were always more women around him than he could possibly handle, so in the evenings we kept him on a short leash. On most days he would rise before dawn, and hike up the snowfield from Timberline Lodge, his skis strapped across his back. From a distance he looked like a medieval bowman. He would climb up past Illumination Rock, and pick his way up the chute beside Crater Rock, all the way to the mountain's summit. Then he would ski all the way down, and be back at the Lodge in time for breakfast. He was very fit, and despite his slight frame, deceptively tough.

Mt. Hood had seen some amazing feats of strength and skill over the years, as well as its fair share of eccentrics. None of us gave much thought to Anselm's early morning jaunts up the mountain—until the great Silvain Saudan arrived in Government Camp, and announced that he was going to ski down from the summit of Mt. Hood for the first time.

Saudan was famous for having skied the edge of the Eiger's North Face the year before, and he was sponsored lavishly by Salomon, one of the leading ski equipment manufacturers. The Oregon press got word of Saudan's coming, and several reporters turned up at Government Camp and Timberline.

Saudan landed in the Timberline car park in a turbine-powered jet-ranger helicopter. He jumped out of the helicopter and was quickly surrounded by camera-clicking media and glamorous-looking women. One of the Timberline instructors grumbled something about a Salomon marketing circus. Saudan chatted to the press, and draped his arms round two of the women for the cameras, while his support crew loaded the chopper up with cameras, skis and other equipment. When the photographers were ready the helicopter lofted Saudan over the roof of the lodge, and up towards the summit of the mountain.

Anselm reached the summit on foot just as Saudan was climbing out of his helicopter. The film crew were very surprised to see him. Anselm was surprised to see them. Saudan, apparently, was annoyed.

The Salomon film crew noticed Anselm's skis and poles, and an animated discussion took place in French on the summit Mt. Hood. Anselm used Rossignol skis with Look Nevada bindings. Both of these companies are big competitors to Salomon.

The Salomon people insisted that Saudan must descend first. They didn't want any tracks to blemish the virgin snow that their man was about to ski for the first time ever. They told Anselm to stay well away from their cameras, and went about setting up their tripods and zoom lenses.

Anselm stood and watched them for a while, nonplussed. When everything was ready Saudan waved his arms about for the cameras, and launched himself off the top of the mountain. The first few hundred feet were confined and tricky, and Saudan picked his way carefully. Some of those watching through binoculars felt that he was overdoing things a bit, exaggerating the jump turns, over-emphasising his pole plants.

Some of these watchers down at Timberline noticed Anselm a hundred yards behind Saudan, skiing altogether more quietly, and following more or less the same route as the great man. It was the route Anselm usually took when he skied down the mountain. Then the watchers saw Saudan stop, and turn and look back. After a minute he carried on, but more carefully than before. This was the point, we discovered later, in Timberline's Rams' Head Bar, where Anselm had called down to Saudan to warn him about the hidden crevasses which lay across his path.

But both skiers made it down to the Lodge without trouble. Saudan hopped into the waiting helicopter, which whisked him off to his next promotional appointment. When we saw the film a few weeks later we noticed that Anselm did not appear in any of the footage, and that Saudan's pause to consider the warning about the crevasses had been artfully edited from the final cut.

The US Ski Instructors' Association decided that Anselm must take their Ski Instructors exam, even though he had been teaching on the mountain all winter. With one thing and another they didn't get around to examining him until April, when the season was more or less over.

It was a rotten day of dark cloud, with rain and snow coming down in soggy, slushy lumps. By the time the examiners turned up to take Anselm out to the Magic Mile for his tests, the slopes were deserted. For an hour Anselm answered their questions, and performed the manoeuvres the examiners asked of him. When they had finished, the examiners huddled together to work out his marks.

Anselm grew bored waiting in the falling rain, and began to play around in the wet snow off to the side of the packed slope. The examiners watched wide-eyed as Anselm danced and cavorted in the heavy, clinging sludge, oblivious to everything else around him.

Later, in the Ram's Head Bar, we overheard one of the examiners talking to Jamie. "I've never seen anything like it," the Examiner said. "The laws of gravity don't seem to apply to him at all; the guy just floated in and out of that heavy crud as if it was feathers." He took a sip of his drink. "It was like watching ballet. Never seen anything like it—I mean I couldn't even get my skis to turn in the stuff.

"When he saw us watching him he got all embarrassed and stopped. When we told him he'd passed the exam, and handed him his instructor's badge and certificate, he thanked us. So we said no, and thanked him for the lesson."

Jamie, working behind the bar, nodded as he cleaned a glass. He'd watched Anselm ski all winter, doing his ethereal ballet in all kinds of conditions.

"It was magic to me, what Anselm did," Jamie told me once. Jamie came from the Azores, where they never have any snow at all.

The Instructor's Race

The ski instructors held a race day at Timberline each spring. All the instructors on the mountain were invited, and the race was taken very seriously. The prize was a small trophy, and a case of beer.

Most of the instructors considered themselves to be pretty good skiers. All of them had the latest equipment, and fancy après-ski fashions, and they spent a good deal of time on weekends, dressed in their colourful instructor's sweaters, chatting to Portland women in the Ram's Head Bar. Bud Nash was the Director of the Timberline Ski School. Bud was a generous fellow, with his feet planted on the ground— but some of his instructors thought they were the cream of the mountain.

The race was due to start in the middle of the afternoon, and one of the instructors set up a difficult giant slalom course on the steepest part of the Pucci run. It was a pretty sight, with banners strung between the gates and the lodge standing behind it, covered in snow. The great south face of the mountain loomed over it all, framing the scene.

The instructors looked over the course, and practiced carving their racing turns. No one was allowed on the course itself. A good crowd had turned up to watch. One or two of the instructors looked as if they might be useful racers, but most of them skied much too prettily—showing lots of form, but not a lot of pace. Sandy thought that some of the instructors might embarrass themselves out on the course.

Ernst turned up at the starting gate in his ancient three-quarter-length canvas coat, just as the starter sent off the pacesetter. Ernst was an old Austrian who ran the lift up on Timberline's Magic Mile. He was a shy man and his English wasn't very good, even though he'd worked up on the mountain for more than twenty years. Ernst never said much to anyone. He and Sandy were friends, but Sandy hardly ever spoke to anyone either.

Ernst's coat was made of stiff, weatherproof material that fell to his knees, and it had a big hood like a monk's cowl. The coat might have been fashionable sometime before the war, and it probably kept him warm and dry when wind-driven sleet howled across the exposed slope at the top of the Mile. But Ernst's coat was the antithesis of every current ski-ing fashion—which consisted of the wet look, the dry look, short, waist-hugging jackets and flared, over-the-boot ski pants. Ernst looked almost palaeolithic beside the healthy young instructors in their fancy outfits.

Ernst waited patiently in the crowd by the starting gate, and watched the instructors race off down the hill. When the last one left the starting gate Ernst stepped forward, and politely asked the Starter if he could take a run down the course.

The starter stared at Ernst for a long minute, taking in the baggy, canvas coat, and lifted his eyes over Ernst's ruddy, weathered face to the floppy, knitted toque on his head. He gazed down at Ernst's battered old wooden skis with their pre-war wire bindings, and the lace-up leather boots on his feet. The starter's face struggled when he reached the bamboo, basket ski poles, and he looked away and coughed.

"It's a pretty difficult course Ernst," the starter said. "I really don't think you should go down it. You might hurt yourself."

Ernst didn't move. He just stood there, and waited for an answer. Someone in the crowd called out, "Go on, let him run the course. Don't be a spoilsport."

The starter, who was one of the senior instructors, shrugged his shoulders. "I guess you can have a go if you really want to Ernst, but don't say I didn't warn you."

Ernst readied himself in the starting gate. It began to snow. His arm in the air, the starter counted him down. At the starter's signal Ernst leaped through the gate and launched himself down the hill, his arms going like pistons, flailing left and right, as if they were fighting through cobwebs made of spun steel. A couple of the watching instructors sniggered.

Ernst smashed through the first gate, destroying it completely—swiping the poles and the banner aside, splaying them across the hillside. Some of the spectators thought he'd crashed, but the more observant ones noted that his skis had passed legally inside the gate poles. Someone in the crowd asked incredulously what he was doing. But Ernst was

230

already far down the course, giving a perfect demonstration of the old Austrian, counter-rotation, ski-ing style.

Ernst battered his way down the mountainside, smashing aside each gate. The spectators shook their heads. None of them had ever seen anything like this demonstration of wild-man, out-of-control skiing. The course Ernst left in his wake looked as if a tornado had been through it, gates and banners scattered to the winds—completely wrecked. When Ernst flashed across the finish line the timekeepers clicked their stopwatches and checked his time, then checked it again, and huddled in conference with each other.

Old Ernst had beaten all the instructors—not by tenths of a second, but by several seconds. They had to give him the Instructors Cup. He took it and waved it at the crowd, and the crowd cheered. Ernst rode up the ski lift with his trophy, and the winner's case of beer, to his post in the little hut at the top of the Miracle Mile, half way up the mountain.

Sandy told me later that Ernst was a member of the Austrian ski team before the war, when he was a young man. He had never mentioned it to anyone else on the mountain. We never did find out what had prompted him to come down from his little box at the top terminal and enter the Instructors' race. But Ernst managed to remind us that it was never a good idea on the mountain to judge anyone by appearances.

The End of the Season

The air gradually lost its sharpness and one day I found that Road 35 was driveable—which meant that I no longer had to park out at the main road, and stumble home in the darkness through snowdrifts. Winter was coming to an end. Soon it would be time to move on.

With the warmer weather some of the ski areas on the south flank of the mountain closed down on weekdays. Multorpor was the first to close, although Ski Bowl, nearby, stayed open during the week for night skiing. Summit Ski School closed down as well, and I lost my instructing job. I got another job working over at Mt. Hood Meadows, running one of the lifts near the lodge.

During the week there were few skiers, and the days were slow and long. One day the trees were full of whiskey jacks. Soon they were joined by little white snowbirds, which came down from the trees and hopped around my feet, picking at the crumbs that fell from my sandwich. Within a few minutes the birds were eating out of my hand. But the job was dull, and it didn't pay much. It was time to figure out what I was going to do next.

I decided to have a party down at the cabin, and managed to scrape up enough money for a keg of beer and some food. It was a fine party, and it lasted all night. Bodies were scattered all over the place in the morning, some of them half frozen; it was still cold up here at night, even if most of the snow had gone.

The carpet was a mess. It had soaked up several times its volume in beer, and had been ground deep with cigarette ash. There was no vacuum in the cabin, and the broom didn't have the horsepower to do the cleaning job.

Sandy scratched his head and said, "I've got an idea."

"What's that?" I couldn't afford to go down to Gresham and rent an industrial carpet cleaner.

"We can throw it in the river for a few days and let the water wash it clean. That'll do it."

"Won't the current wash it away?" I gazed at the Zig-zag River, racing full of bright snowmelt past the back deck, bouncing over its rocky bed.

"Not if we tie a rope to it, and wrap the rope round a tree. That'll hold it down."

It sounded like the answer.

We woke up the others and rolled up the carpet. It was heavy; it took six of us to carry it out the back door, and onto the riverbank. We looped ropes around two of the carpet's corners, and hitched them to two sturdy trees. Then we dropped the carpet off the little bridge, into the river. The

Zigzag River isn't wide, but it comes nearly all the way from the top of the mountain and it was running very fast.

We left the carpet in the river for a week. I peered into the waters every day to see if the torrent was scouring the dirt out of it, but the river was white with foam, and rising higher as the temperature went up. I decided that it was time to haul the carpet out, and asked the partygoers to come back to the cabin to help.

We took up the strain on the ropes, but the carpet was waterlogged, and far too heavy for the six of us to pull out of the river. Sandy scratched his head. The others sat down. Sandy usually managed to think of something.

"Anyone bring any beer?" asked one of the helpers.

"We can't leave it in the river. We've got to get it out." I was starting to panic at the thought of the cabin's owner asking about his expensive carpet.

"The river runs dry about August," said someone helpfully.

We tried again, straining at the ropes, but the carpet wouldn't budge. It was completely saturated with water, and the current was much too strong. A rugby team couldn't have pulled it out.

We opened up the beer and sat down. It was pleasant to sit on the step of the back deck, with spring sunshine slanting through the trees. But I could feel the collective will ebbing slowly away.

A yellow Oregon Telephone Company truck rumbled gingerly along Road 35, one of the first vehicles to come down since the plough cleared away the snow. Sandy jumped up and ran out in front of the truck, and put the case of beer down on the road. The truck stopped and the driver climbed down from his cab. Sandy told him about the carpet in the river. The lineman accepted the beer right away. The two telephone company men put their small crane to work on the problem, and pulled the carpet out of the river in five minutes. They even manoeuvred the truck off the road, so that they could help us drape the carpet over the rail of the deck to dry.

The carpet sat on the deck rail for two weeks before it was dry enough to go back in the cabin. When we carried it inside, it was almost spotless.

Brookings

Last night I sat at Samoa's *stern and watched the dying sun for a long, long time, thinking about home. I watched the sun go down behind the trees on the hillside across the harbour. A flight of herring gulls flew through the evening sky to the sea, which is a good sign for the weather for the next few days. Slash fires were burning up on the hill and the smoke rose up purple and straight, and it was all reflected in the water in front of me. A late fishing boat came in over the black water, rippling the reflections in its wake, and as it went by the deck man looked over and waved . . . and that was rather fine.*

—Diary: July 16, 1971

236

Mez offers me deckhand work for the summer on a troller down the Oregon coast. I tell him I'll take it; it's the only work around. Mez works in Bud Valian's ski shop during the winter, and does some ski instructing on weekends. Like many of the people on Mt. Hood, he has to find other work between ski seasons. Mez is a solid, reliable sort; a trained engineer from Minnesota, who sometimes works as a rigger on the high Hydro towers.

Before I go fishing, though, I have to go down to San Francisco to meet my friend Sheena from Edinburgh. I promised to take her up to Mt. Hood, where she's been offered a summer job. I drive down through central Oregon on back roads, until I reach Interstate 5 at the California border. The little Triumph sports car likes the bright California sunshine, so I stop and put the hood down, and don't stop again until I've crossed the Bay Bridge. Sheena is waiting for me at one of the residences at San Francisco State University. She comes down to the lobby with her bag, I turn the car around, and we drive north up the coast road—out of California and up through Oregon—until it's time to turn east for Mt. Hood. Buffy has a spare room ready, and Sheena's job is waiting for her in the restaurant at Timberline Lodge.

After I drop Sheena at the mountain, I head back across northern Oregon to US 101, and drive down the coast. US 101—Highway 1, the finest road in the whole of North America. It stretches down the coast, hazy with sea mist, undulates past fields and forests, headlands and harbours, winds along beside deserted sandy beaches. Little towns are scattered all the way down the coast; towns like Fourmile, Sixes, Port Orford, Pistol River. All of them have small, dead-end bars, with red neon signs in the windows winking Blitz, or Bud, or Coors. Taverns, the Americans call them—

as if they're trying to evoke something homey. All of them seem to have a burl clock on the wall, a jar of pickled eggs on the counter, jerky and stale peanuts stapled to a board behind the bar; all of them sell the same, watery beer, play the same lonesome songs on the jukebox. Each one of them exudes a faint scent of desperation, of life passing by, the air inside thick with the toasted tobacco smoke of Marlboros, or Luckies.

Young people hardly ever go into these places, and the clientele looks as if it has been sitting inside for years. The women are adept at pool, and they'll take money off you if you take them on. They're middle-aged—like the men—with high, early-sixties hair, and they have this façade of toughness. They like to sound harder as they get older, and they drop the last syllables from their words and say things like ". . . still rainin' outside?" And get an answering, monosyllabic ". . . Yeah."

Or ". . . ain't yew buyin' t'night, Artie? Look'd like a moth ah saw flyin' outta yer wallet there . . . as big as a bird it was…" They seem to cultivate this lack of refinement, perhaps to deter thoughts of what might have been.

I have to meet up with Mez in Brookings, a small fishing port just above the Oregon-California border, where the Brookings River empties into the Pacific. Brookings is a tough little town, with a harbour filled with all shapes of fishing boats, and a wild pub of its own sitting out on the wharf.

Our boat is a thirty-nine-foot troller called *Samoa*, and Mez is fishing it for the summer, under contract. *Samoa* is grey, with faded maroon trim, and badly in need of paint. Something is always breaking on board, and we spend a lot of time at an untidy supplies shop in the hills behind town, rooting around for engine parts, gurdy bits, shackles and stays and rigging.

We live on the boat. It's cramped and damp, with a pair of bunks wedged tightly into the bow, and a small cluttered cabin with a stove and table. It's hard to keep clean, and we share the boat with a range of tiny bugs and creatures.

We spend most of our days trolling up and down the coast, searching for fish. All the fishermen have theories about where to find fish and how to catch them, and every theory is different. We don't catch much, and we spend most of our slim takings on repairs to the boat. After a while we decide to shadow one of the highliners—one of the top fishermen—and put our lines down when he does.

We've been following our highliner for a week and we haven't caught any more fish than we usually do, so we buy him drinks in the pub, try to pump him for tips. But he wants to talk about other things.

"See that guy up there?" He nods at a stocky man with curly hair and a thick neck, sitting up on a stool at the bar. The man's sleeves are rolled up tight above his biceps. "He'll start to get loud when he's had a drink. You wanna steer clear of him. He got real strange after Viet Nam. He was in the Green Berets out there, out in the jungle all by his-self for a long time. Good fisherman . . . but you stay clear of him—yes-sir, good an' clear."

The highliner chews slowly on a toothpick, watching the man at the bar. A tattoo on the ex-Green Beret's forearm shines dully in the smoky light; a snake wound around a dagger, its head drawn back to strike. We ask the highliner what gear he uses.

"White hoochies on the deep line," he says, without moving his eyes from the man at the bar, "fire-engine-red spoons on the surface for silvers." Silvers are what the Americans call the coho salmon.

The ex-Green Beret orders two bottles of Budweiser from the barman, and sits with one in each fist, drinking from one, then the other.

"I never change up my gear," continues the highliner, "an' I always watch the water temperature. Salmon swim in forty-three degree water. You don't find them in forty-four degrees, or in forty-two. They're particular 'bout the temperature and there's no point in putting your lines down where there ain't no fish."

We don't know if he's telling us the truth or not, but he's got sophisticated sounding and scanning equipment on his boat, and expensive thermometers. And we know he catches a lot of fish. It's good of him to share his secrets.

The next day we take a trip up to the supplies shop in the hills behind town, and come back to the boat with a box of white hoochies and a box of red spoons. When we go out fishing we watch our highliner like a hawk. We load up our lines with the brand new hoochies and spoons, and put them down when he drops his, and trail him up and down the coast like shadows. He doesn't seem to mind, and waves across at us from time to time. We can see him flipping fish onto his boat as if they're coming off a conveyor belt. But the little bells on the springs at the end of our lines stay resolutely silent.

Because *Samoa* is so unreliable we day-fish most of the time. This means getting up early in the morning. A few other boats go out with us then, but most of the fleet sails off for days at a time. The big shoals are usually further out than we can fish on day trips.

The air is thick and heavy just before dawn, the deck slick with dew. The sky is clammy and overcast, hanging over the harbour like a coat. A couple of other boats are getting ready to go out, the deckhands moving quietly about like me, loosening the mooring ropes, checking the lines, making sure the weights and paravanes are tied down.

The first engine noise stabs into the grey dark and a boat two fingers over slides out into the channel, its diesel engine settling to a quiet throbbing, the red and green nav lights on her stubby mast cutting a line along the black hill across the harbour. Mez nods and says okay and I unhook the mooring rope, pull it on board and untie it from the deck cleat. It can go below until we need it to tie up tonight.

Samoa moves away from the wharf, rocking the other boats with a gentle wake as she moves past them into the channel. A breeze blows over the deck. It's raw, this morning air, and it smells of the sea, a rich penetrating smell of salt and wet and decay and life all at the same time. It makes me shiver, and brings me alive.

"Coffee's up," calls Mez from the cabin, and I step inside where it's warm.

A rumour floats around the pub one night that tuna fish are running up north, a long way offshore. Briefly we contemplate going out after them, for there's good money in tuna. The fishermen bounce feathers fast over the surface of the water to attract the tuna, and catch them on barbless hooks, flicking them over their shoulders into the hold. There's an art to it. One of the guys in the pub tells us that a good deckhand can catch tuna almost as quickly as you can count them.

In the end we decide to stick to salmon because tuna means changing up our gear again, and we don't have the money to do that. We decide to try fishing further up the coast though; go out for a few days this time. Our timing could be better.

We motor north to a place called Mac Arch, a huge sea rock with a hole through its middle. *Samoa's* engine pounds away all day, shivering the hull with vibrations. Iron Mike— the automatic pilot—has the helm, keeping us on a track well outside the headlands.

There aren't many secure night anchorages on this stretch of the Oregon coast, but there's a small, partially sheltered bay behind Mac Arch, just off the shore. It's the only place to hide on miles of rocky coast, and it's tricky to get in and out of. But it's only safe when the wind isn't blowing from the west or the southwest, and these are the prevailing winds here. Saw-tooth rocks reach a long way out to sea from the headlands on either side of Mac Arch, encouraging us not to make mistakes.

We fish off Mac Arch for two days. Things are going well. We're catching a lot of fish, and then a storm blows in. It's a classic west coast storm, which they'd call a small hurricane in most other places—the kind of storm that convinces sceptics that the Oregon coast is a dangerous place. It convinces us. In less than an hour we're fighting waves thirty feet high.

The wind rises quickly over a dark green sea. At first it spins out white spray in a cold, soaking rain, but soon it's whipping great lumps of water off the tops of the waves, smashing them against *Samoa's* cabin windows. The backsides of the crests are white with froth, the troughs alive with green, snaking veins. The heavy lead weights we use to sink

242

the lines break away from their beds at the stern, and start swinging about like wrecking balls, smashing into the gurdies and steel lines, splintering the bulwarks.

Mez edges out of the cabin to tie the weights down in their holders. I've got the wheel and the throttle, and then I see an enormous black roller towering above the others, bearing down on us at a terrific speed. I shout over my shoulder at Mez, but I can see he doesn't have time to make it back to the cabin. I crank the power on full, to try and make it over the top of the wave before it can turn us back and flip us over.

At the top of the wave, I pull the power all the way off, at the exact moment to stop us flying off the crest and burying ourselves in the next one and driving ourselves down to the bottom. But still the crest's too sharp for *Samoa*; she hangs on its edge, balanced for a long, long second like an acrobat on a rope, and then she gives a shudder and falls off into the trough. The trough's a deep hole with sheer sides and we fall down and down and the next wave towers overhead, and then it hits. The water goes dark and green-black. The front of *Samoa's* cabin caves in towards me and water sprouts through the seams at the edges of the windscreen glass and I know we're not going to come back up.

But after an age *Samoa* breaks through to grey light on the other side. I'm sure Mez has gone overboard and there's no way I'll ever find him in this wild sea, with the light going fast. But there he is, soaked with icy seawater, staggering through the spray to the cabin, his clothes sticking to him like shrink-wrap. The wave picked him up like a toy and hurled him against the gurdy davits and pinned him there. It was just enough to stop him from being swept off the boat.

243

We shut everything down, turn the boat around so our tail is to the weather, and toss out a storm anchor, which holds us like a parachute. We also throw out two trailing lines, in case one of us goes over the side. Then we inspect the boat carefully for damage. The rogue wave has hit *Samoa* a tremendous blow, and we're taking on water. Two boards have sprung at the bow; more water is coming in than the pump can handle. We work furiously at it, and in a while it starts to look as if we'll just about make it back to harbour, as long as nothing else goes wrong.

We have to take it slowly in order not to stress the boat any more, but we eventually make it back to Brookings. Several of *Samoa's* seams have ruptured along the front of the cabin, as well as up at the bow. *Samoa* is battered and bruised, but she's still afloat, and she's saved our bacon.

A Summer Run

The verdict at the boatyard is that *Samoa* has to be laid up for two weeks for repairs, so I decide to take a few days off, and drive up to Mt. Hood. It's high summer, and the Willamette Valley is ripe with wheat. When I reach the mountain I find that the snow has gone from Government Camp. The air on the mountain is warm and sleepy, as if the village is in hibernation, waiting for next winter before it can come alive again.

The next morning I get up early, and hitch a ride up the mountain with Jamie, on one of the Timberline Snow Kats. Jamie takes the Kat straight up, above the Miracle Mile, past the ruin of Silcox Hut, and up the Palmer Snowfield to Crater Rock. He lets me off somewhere above the ten thousand foot mark, less than a thousand feet below the summit.

It's a beautiful, clear morning. Oregon is stretched out at my feet, its distances magnified in the morning air. The Cascade Mountains are clear and fresh as far as I can see, as if I can reach out and touch them all. The silence is perfect, crystal. The great volcanic peaks rise up to the south—Jefferson, the Three Sisters, the smudge of Shasta on the horizon. I can see the whole length of the state.

I have the perfect skis for this run, a pair of Rossignol Allais Majors that I've bought from Bud Valian. They're long and flexible; stable, supple and sensitive—giant slalom skis, two hundred and fifteen centimetres in length, and perfect for the steep, sweeping snowfield below me.

Very quickly, I pick up tremendous speed. The run will be over far too quickly at this rate, and so I swoop over to Illumination Rock and stop to drink in the view over its shoulder, to the west. As I glance over the huge, turreted rock above me, something metallic catches the sun. It's a little remembrance plaque for Joe Leuthold, screwed into the stone—a small memorial for a respected guide, in this lonely place, high on the mountain.

Then I'm off down to Timberline Lodge far below—wide turns and some choppy shortswing, flying down the fine-grained snow. Oregon rushes up towards me. It's the run of a lifetime.

Fishing Again

We take *Samoa* down the coast of northern California as far as Cape Mendocino, and slowly work our way a hundred miles offshore. The weather is warm and we're fishing on our own; no other boats have come out as far as this. Day after day the sea is calm and glassy. We have a good stereo system on board, and some fine music to play, and sometimes it seems as if we're the only people left on earth.

Every morning, just before sunrise, we put our lines down through a translucent surface mist. We cut slab steaks from the back of the first small fish we catch, and pop them in the frying pan for breakfast, with chopped onions, sliced potatoes, and lots of pepper. Every week or so we sail into Eureka or Crescent City to sell our fish, make repairs and get ice. As soon as we can, we head out again.

ↄ

We're trolling patiently through the morning mist, looking for salmon, when an enormous tail rises silently out of the water beside the boat. It's wider across than the whole length of *Samoa*, standing up beside us like a gigantic hand, no more than ten feet away. The whale's tail slides back below the surface without a ripple, without a sound. Neither of us says a word. There's nothing to be said.

The sight of that great animal so close in that ghostly, elemental setting crystallises the thoughts in my mind; it's time to move on again.

Samoa's engine begins churning oil into her bilge soon after we turn back for Brookings. Mez is forced to lay the boat up for a complete engine re-build, and that's the end of her summer. I've got just enough money to drive north and collect my things from Mt. Hood.

LA to New York

Things looked grim from where we were standing, in the middle of the Mojave Desert. The road ran razor-straight on either side of us as far as we could see, across dead flat sand and scrub. The sun had just gone down and all that was left was a fading glow in the sky to the west. Nothing stirred; absolutely nothing. The silence was palpable. In minutes it would be dark as only the desert can be dark.

We'd left Pasadena that afternoon and hitched two rides. The first one took us up to Barstow in the hills—a sort of bleak, no-hoper town that looked like a disused movie set from 'Hud', or 'Paris, Texas'. It sits at the junction of highways to Las Vegas and Bakersfield and LA, and points east.

A big black pickup truck provided our second ride. The guy had seen Helène before he saw me, and he was pissed off when I hopped into the cab beside her. He didn't say anything, but the tension was thick. He drove fast out into the desert without a word for nearly an hour, and then he said, "I'm on the wrong road. Ya gotta get out here." He jumped on the brakes and the tires screamed to a stop, then he leaned over and opened the door and more or less threw us out, reaching a long arm round to the box and tossing our bags after us. We stood and watched him take off across a quarter mile or so of dirt and scrub to where the westbound lane headed back towards Barstow. When the sound of the truck finally died away, we knew we were stuck.

We sat there for an hour, and then another and another and no cars came by. We might have been the only people on earth. The stars hung overhead like a magic carpet, and twinkled in more millions than either of us had ever seen before, raised as we were within the cast of cities and street lights. It became cold, as only the desert can be at night. And still it was silent, as it must have been out there through the ages.

Then, away off to the west and so faint that I thought I'd imagined it, I heard a sound. "Listen," I said. "There's something coming." We strained our ears.

"It might be thunder," said Helène. The sound came again, this time a little more certain. It was low down the audio scale, but insistent: not a noise from nature. "It's a big truck," she said.

Over the next few minutes it grew, until we could distinguish a deep, throaty grumbling. "Sounds like a tank," I said. We stood up, and stared into the night. There was not a glimmer of light, and no horizon to be seen. We stood for what seemed like hours. Then, far, far off in the night came two little pinpricks of light, and the noise grew as whatever it was moved towards us.

It was Danny, hurtling across the desert night.

Danny stopped when he saw Helène in his headlights. She's tall and her hair blew in the desert wind. She is fair and strong and she must have seemed to him like the Swedish apparition she was, in the middle of that empty desert. He didn't seem to mind when I popped up beside her.

"We'll have to do some sorting out," he said, and moved a couple of bags into the small space behind his seat. "There ain't much room in here."

Danny's car was a Pontiac. The front two-thirds of it was taken up by a massive hood, under which sat one of the biggest engines in the US. A small trunk, and the driver's cockpit—for that's what it was—took up the remainder.

When he had us stowed inside with our bags, Danny introduced himself. "Ah'm from Tennessee," he drawled, "the Smokies." His handshake was firm, and unlike our last ride, his eyes lingered only slightly longer on Helène than they did on me.

Danny told us he was returning home from San Francisco. Home, but first he had to make a detour to Washington. "Muh brother got wedded, and it took a day or two more'n ah figured it would. So now ah'm in a hurry," he went on, "an' if you' all will drive in the night, ah'll drive in the daytime. That way we don't hev to make no stops 'cept fer somethin' to eat 'n to gas up."

When it was my turn to drive Danny explained the controls. "Don't touch this one," he said, gently tapping a lever which stuck out of the floor. "It drops oil out the sump onto the road. Or this one," he placed his hand on another. "It'll dump the whole load." He looked at me for a moment. "From the tank. There's a two hundred gallon tank under here, bolted onto the chassis. At home we fill it up with moonshine and run it down from the hills."

"The Smokies?" I asked. I'd heard stories, but they'd sounded like fiction to me.

"Yeah. This here Pontiac can outrun any police car in any state in the Union." He said it quietly, matter-of-factly.

"Is that what you were doing in San Francisco then? Delivering a load of moonshine."

Danny laughed. "No. We never take it that far," he said. "I was strictly out there visitin' my brother. An' his new wife."

I took my place behind the wheel. Danny curled up in the passenger seat and closed his eyes and went to sleep in seconds. Helène was squeezed into the tiny space behind the two seats, with my green duffle bag for a pillow. In front of me stretched the longest hood I'd ever seen. It seemed to fill the whole road. When I fired up the engine it reverberated through the steering wheel and the driver's seat, until it settled down to a regular throbbing roar, like a giant's heartbeat. I let out the clutch and in seconds we were flying along at eighty miles an hour, and then a hundred and more. In those days few states had speed limits.

I drove down the night, through Arizona and into New Mexico, following the track laid out by the Pontiac's headlights.

And it was in the sky, and not upon the earth that I was surprised to find a change. Explain it how you may . . . the sun rises with a different splendour in America and Europe. There is more clear gold and scarlet in our old country mornings; more purple,

252

brown and smoky orange in those of the new . . .
it has a duskier glory, and more nearly resembles
sunset . . .

—Robert Louis Stevenson
The Amateur Immigrant

Daylight revealed a road which ran endlessly past mesquite
and rock, and sand-soil of unrelenting grey-ochre colours.
It ran straight without corners, and flat without hills or undulations of any kind. All there was, was the horizon, which
kept a kind of pace with the car, receding steadily as we drove
on and on towards it. The morning found us coasting past
Navajo reservations and occasional billboards, until at last
we came to a downward slope, which dropped us towards
Albuquerque. We passed through the city's grey outskirts,
and then climbed up and slowly out of New Mexico, and on
across the neck of Texas. Amarillo came and went, and we
raced on up the southern prairie, stopping occasionally to
fill Danny's thirsty car with gasoline.

The weather changed from dry to wet right at the Oklahoma border, and the air smelled suddenly of damp soil and
musky prairie grasses. That night we stopped for a snack in
Oklahoma City and nearly got in a fight with some local
rednecks who didn't like strangers. The next morning found
us on the outskirts of Little Rock, Arkansas, a place famous
for its early '60's civil rights associations, its air sweet and
thick with perfumes of honeysuckle and jasmine.

Soon we were in the upper Mississippi delta lands: flat
and endless, dead-straight roads all the way to Memphis.
Big-girdered bridges were strung across the great brown river, and for the first time since I'd been in the US I saw streets
full of black people. Now we were in Tennessee, and slowly

253

climbing out of the Mississippi basin. Nashville came and went, surrounded by old tire dumps and a straggling litter of commerce and highway signs.

Knoxville sat among lakes at the edge of the Appalachian mountain range, and then we were in among the Smokies, on back roads with tumbledown farms and shacks and broken machinery. This was Danny's country and he obviously knew it well. It was a place of little valleys, locked away among high, wooded mountains that the rest of the world seemed to have passed by. The countryside was mysterious and unkempt, and linked together by narrow, winding roads. On the surface it was peaceful, and even pretty in a decayed sort of way. But I could feel that it held an edge; that it was somehow pinched and threatening, and that the people who lived here kept their distance and held secrets.

The next morning, dawn came up among the rolling foothills of West Virginia and showed us small, neat fields. Most of the farmhouses were still asleep, but this was horse country, and Appaloosas, Arab crosses and stocky quarter horses grazed the dewy grass, their flanks shining in the gentle morning light.

> . . . the contours of the land were soft and English. It was not quite England, neither was it quite France; yet like enough either to seem natural in my eyes.
> —Robert Louis Stevenson
> *The Amateur Immigrant*

Here on the eastern slopes of the Appalachians the farms were prosperous and well kept. They weren't hard-worked and broken, and dusty and battered, like the farms on the other side of the mountains. These were tidy like hobby farms, drifted with a light mist, between fresh-painted fences.

We reached Washington before nine, during the morning rush hour. "This is it," said Danny as we drove up to a bridge at a place called Alexandria. "This is the Potomac. I'm heading off here. Got people to see; things to do." He pulled over to the side of the road, and we said our goodbyes and stepped out into the seething traffic.

We had crossed the country from the Pacific almost to the Atlantic coast between Friday evening and Monday morning. But we weren't finished yet. We still had to make our way up to New York. A car stopped and we hopped in. The driver was going to Baltimore. He dropped us on the freeway at the edge of the city and within seconds a stern policeman drew up.

"Better show me some ID," he said, and then, "You can't hitch-hike here. It's against the law to hitch-hike on the freeway." He scrutinised our passports. "You're not from around here," he said, and told us to hop in his cruiser. Right away I noticed the two guns. A short-barrelled shotgun rested just under the dashboard; a heavy calibre Remington automatic was clipped under the front seat. But the policeman was friendly enough, and told us he'd take us to a place where we'd stand a better chance of picking up a ride. He was true to his word, and after he dropped us off we stood for less than five minutes before a blue Chevrolet stopped. Behind the wheel sat a young man in uniform, no older than myself.

Tim was a deserter from the US Army. He told us this as soon as he figured out that we weren't American. I asked him why he was wearing a uniform. "They check your ID if you're in civvies," he said. "They never ask someone in uniform. If they ever do check me out, they'll find me in the files and they'll know right away I'm AWOL. Then I'm in big trouble." He glanced over at me. "I bet you've had your ID checked while you've been in the States. You're the right age. You'd be in 'Nam if you were American."

He was right of course. Often over the past few weeks I'd had my ID checked by the police in Oregon and California; even earlier that morning in Maryland. I'd thought nothing of it at first, putting it down to the normal paranoia of US officialdom. But then, as I got to know people in California, I found that most of the young men lived in fear that their names would come up in the weekly lottery draw for the draft.

Tim saw me eyeing the single tab on his lapel. "I made myself a Lieutenant too," he said softly. "They don't expect officers to desert."

"Was it that bad over there?" I asked him. He stared straight ahead at the road for so long that I thought he hadn't heard me. He sucked at his cheek, drawing it into a big hollow.

"It's pretty bad," he said quietly. "I did a long tour and now they want me to go back for more." He pointed to his cheek; the one he'd been sucking in. "See this?" A dark mark reached from near the corner of his mouth, up under his eye. I'd noticed it as soon as we got in the car. It was the same on both sides of his face. "I took a gook bullet through here an' it went right through an' came out the other side. Didn't touch a thing 'cept the skin. Didn't even take a tooth out." He rubbed it dreamily. "But it was way too close for me. No sir. I ain't goin' back there."

We skirted Philadelphia, and before lunch New York's skyline came in view. "There you go," said Tim. "We're in

256

Jersey now. You can get a bus from here, or a train. You'll be in Manhattan in no time."

Helène and I got out, and Tim drove off towards a black-edged sky in his upright, blue car. I thought I heard distant thunder. But when we turned to look across the river the towers and buttresses of the city were bright with mid-day sunshine.

Two Worlds

Writing-On-Stone

The prairie wind spins through long grasses and scrub cactus, ruffles the surface of the water hole, picks at the hair on the antelope's back like a wandering thought. She lifts her head from drinking, and looks around to make sure she's alone.

It's there most of the time, this inquisitive prairie wind—pushing, testing, exploring. But by the end of summer you've learned that it's a good thing; it keeps down the bugs, the black flies and mosquitoes; freshens the air after the heat of the day.

Away in the distance the Rocky Mountains are no more than a smudge, a suggestion on the horizon. More tangible are heaped piles of black cumulo-nimbus, spitting sparks as they gather and begin to advance slowly out from the west.

∾

Donald Finlayson and Elizabeth McKenzie sailed from Caithness in the north of Scotland on June 20th, 1850. They were bound for Canada on the barque *Argo*, registered in Stettin on the Baltic. Donald began work on August 26th, 1850 in Dundas, Canada West (now Ontario). Donald was my great-great-grandfather's brother. I'd always thought that I was the first one from my family to pull up stakes and migrate to North America. It was a long time before I found out that I wasn't.

Donald and Elizabeth had four sons—James, Donald, Charles and Thomas. On October 6th, 1873, twenty-two year old James Finlayson enlisted at Toronto in the newly formed North West Mounted Police. He was assigned to B Troop, which left Fort Garry, Manitoba the following summer on a trek across the prairies. Their task was to establish law and order between the Manitoba boundary and the Rocky Mountains. B Troop was part of a force of three hundred men with freight wagons, oxcarts, cattle for food, field guns, mortars, and an assortment of farm machinery. This was the beginning of Canada's Mounted Police Force, and the start of the journey that the Mounties now refer to as "The Great Trek".

Em and I have come out here to see if we can piece together some of James Finlayson's wanderings with the North West Mounted Police that long ago summer, when the Mounties were the first representatives of Canada's government to travel this way. We've come to see if we can draw any connections across the best part of a hundred and thirty years—connections between the old world and the new, conjugations of character or spirit.

৩

It is brittle country, this prairie. The grass is thin, the soil hard and cracked, and dried out by the warm summer winds. A lump of earth crumbles through my fingers; blows away as dust. Before the rains come this land is right on the edge of desert. Without water it will be volatile, unreliable, easily barren.

The landscape is as flat as a plank. Except for small undulations it's like sitting on top of an upturned plate. All afternoon we watch storms travelling portentously about the prairie like great battleships, plodding dangerously out from the horizon, drifting close as if they're searching us out, moving away again.

During the month of June 1874, as the Mounties moved slowly south from Lower Fort Garry to Dufferin, near the Boundary Road—a recently surveyed track which followed the US-Canada border and offered the only decent trail to the west—they began to sort themselves out. James was made teamster, although he had almost no experience with horses. But he liked them, and his appointment seems to have come because of his success in recovering most of the two hundred and fifty horses which had stampeded from the Mounties' encampment one night during a violent electrical storm. Early in July the Mounties were ready to move westwards. They would be on the trail until the first snows came in the fall.

Big, black clouds gather in front of the mountains as the light begins to fade. They advance slowly, like cavalry. Then they're upon us, spitting and sparking, lashing the land with cracks of thunder. We secure the tents, set up a tarpaulin, pour wine. Em's cousin Joe has a fire going, smoky with wet wood. Already he's turned the tarp into a cookhouse. Joe has planned out every one of the meals for the days we're going to spend out on the prairie.

There are half a dozen of us here, far out on the plains, a long way from any city. The others are from my Canadian family; they're prairie-bred, versed in the extravagant tempers of this landscape, always curious about its fragile history. We're camped in a tiny, remote campsite surrounded by rangeland, a nearby waterhole the temporary home to sandhill cranes and other migratory birds.

The rain fills the air as if it's trying to remove the oxygen, coming down thick in sheets, racked by blasts of sudden wind until we can see no more than a few feet. Water flows over the dry ground in a silvery carpet. Even though the soil has a sandy texture it cannot absorb such a vast amount of moisture. Night falls, and we bring out lamps and candles, pour more wine, and create a dry, lighted place among the wild elements. For supper, Joe produces rich tacos—concoctions of seasoned ground beef wrapped with tomatoes and lettuce in flour tortillas.

July 12th, 1874—Saturday
Rained heavy during the first part of last night. Struck tents and marched twelve miles. Camped in a nice open plain with plenty of wood and water. Grasshoppers here in clouds, so that we could hardly see the sun. Heavy rain and hail-storm in the evening.

July 14th—Tuesday
Very windy with lots of dust. Camped on the open plain near a

swamp. No water, no wood, no supper. The bull train did not get in till after midnight, therefore no provisions.

July 16th—Thursday
One Slap Jack per man for breakfast; lucky to get that. On the march at 5.30 a.m. Arrived at Turtle Mountain after dark and camped near a small stream. Had supper on the same as I had for dinner, namely Nothing!!

At night the sky is deep with stars. Em's cousin Jack sets up a portable telescope and starts searching for the Andromeda galaxy. When he eventually finds it, he places it in the middle of the eyeglass, where it sits like a fuzzy ball of wool. He calls us out to look, and then we allow ourselves to be distracted by a thin moon, and reach out to it through Jack's powerful lens, as if we can touch its dusty, flour-like surface.

Food was a continual problem. From time to time the Mounties could find it on the prairie—shoot wild birds or antelope, as they travelled west—but there was rarely enough of it, and sometimes they had to go without. These privations led to desertions among the men, but things were much more serious for the horses. Commissioner French, the officer in charge of the expedition, had selected finely-bred Ontario horses for the journey—smart, good-looking animals, used to feeding on oats and soft, cultivated foods. French's horses wouldn't eat the coarse prairie grass, and much effort was expended in carrying feed along—until it ran out.

August 4th, 1874—Tuesday
Reveille at 3 a.m. On the march at 5 a.m. Marched all day over a barren Prairie. Many of the horses used up. No wood. Had

to cook our supper with buffalo chips. Colonel McLeod left us today with ten men for Wood Mountain for a supply of pemmican. Marched today thirty miles.

August 6th—Thursday
Remained all day in camp. Had a good feed of frogs. Weather fine.

Em and I have left our prairie campsite. We've been following the Mounties for several days, making a generous loop down from the north to pick up their trail because we've come out of the west, and they came from the civilised east. But there is little now to mark their passage.

A few signs denote the Red Coat trail, pitched across southern Saskatchewan at the side of dusty farm tracks, along the dead-straight dirt roads. Most of the signs are pockmarked and chipped, as if some passing hunter has used them for target practice. We drive through tiny villages like Cadillac, Admiral, and Scotsguard, fill up with gasoline at dusty wayside garages hung with old hubcaps and licence plates, and stocked with spare parts for cars and tractors that haven't been seen on these roads for forty years. The houses in these prairie towns are tidy and small, with tiny windows to cool their interiors from the summer heat and protect them from the icy cold in winter.

James would have seen little change in the landscape from one day to the next; the eternal prairie rolling away to its horizons, like the North Sea off the top of Scotland, where his father had grown up.

August 11th, 1874—Tuesday

Cloudy and chilly. Many of the horses gave up. Had one horse gave out with me. I had to unharness and let him feed for two hours before I could reach noon camp. First signs of buffalo and Indians today. B Troop was left here as rear guard. Marched two miles and camped in a beautiful green valley with a large swamp affording good grazing for our horses. No wood. Cooked our meal with buffalo chips. On picquet tonight.

August 13th—Thursday

A camp of Sioux Indians about one mile from us. Several of them came to our camp today to see what they could get. A large tent was pitched to hold a Powwow in. The trumpeters played a note for them. Then they got some presents from Colonel French. Beautiful weather.

The Mounties were lost much of the time, lacking faith in guides who didn't know the country west of the Dirt Hills, which lie near the present Manitoba-Saskatchewan border. They meandered back and forth across the prairie, mistaking one river for another miles away to the north, or the south, or the west. There were never enough supplies, although they managed to eat quite well from time to time after they encountered the buffalo.

August 22nd, 1874—Saturday

Colonel Macleod left with thirty ox carts for White Mud River after more oats. Today we passed a halfbreed train which was searched for liquor but found none. Passed through some beautiful scenery. Country very hilly. We had to carry grass with us as the buffalo have been through here and left it bare. The advance guard saw a herd. I saw a dead one with the hide on for the first time. Hard work for the cooks as the buffalo chips are wet and will not burn.

An enormous amount of energy had to go into feeding the horses, whose Ontario stomachs couldn't adapt to the wild prairie grasses. One by one these precious animals wasted away and died. Without horses to carry them across the prairie the expedition would be lost. But when Colonel McLeod, a practical man, returned from a provisioning trip with some tough Indian ponies, French ordered him to turn them loose. They were too scruffy for his command.

The Cypress Hills sit just north of the United States border, where the provinces of Saskatchewan and Alberta meet. They rise out of the plains green and treed, fresh with streams of clear-running water, temperate and forgiving after the harsh prairie. When the Mounties came upon the Cypress Hills after weeks of flatland, dirt and stones and scrub prairie vegetation, they must have seemed like an oasis. Here at least the men and horses would have plenty of water and food. These hills had long been favoured by Indians, and the wild game from here had filled their larders for centuries. The jackpine made good tipi poles, and the hides of buffalo and grizzly bear provided warm, watertight coverings and blankets, winter clothing, healing potions, and valued ornamentations.

The Cypress Hills are well farmed now, and white Charolais crosses and Black Angus roam broad, fenced pastures—valuable, sophisticated livestock, a long way from the oxen and skinny range cattle that started out with the settlers who built the crumbling old homesteads which still dot the landscape. These old pioneer buildings stand creaking in the fields. Porous wooden barns and roofless cabins lean over creeks, rotted out by the hard winters that visit this place. Gophers, attracted by the sound of the car, pop out of holes in the dirt road, and dive out of sight when they see danger bearing down on them.

August 25th, 1874—Tuesday
Marched until 2 p.m. when we camped. We passed some beautiful scenery. High, hilly country with no wood. We are camped by a little lake called "Duck Lake". We have to march in scarlet tunics with belts on, and carbine close to hand. We also got twenty rounds more ammunition. Looks like business. Weather fine with wind.

August 26th—Wednesday
We are in a stationary camp for a few days until Col. Macleod arrives with his train. We are camped on the Cypress Hills. Weather fine.

Brazen Richardson's squirrels wake us early, attacking the tent, stealing our food. We're camped in a cool forest, in a crook of Battle Creek. Water chatters easily past the flap of the tent. It has been a long night, the darkness busy with strange sounds of splashing and snuffling, animals drinking from the creek, coyote howls.

After supper last night we walked away from the camp under a thin moon, and were quickly enveloped by the wildness of the hills, and the subtle noises of small animals rustling through the long grasses beside the track, by the call of night birds and the hooting of owls. It was cool for midsummer—chill enough to wear a sweater—but sudden currents brushed us with quick warm breezes, and bent the wild sunflowers at the side of the track. It was not hard then to imagine the night airs realigned by the passing spirits of the people who once lived here, hunted these hills.

Battle Creek winds through the green heart of the Cypress Hills, and slides through spacious forests of lodgepole pine before it descends into a wide grassy bowl at the Fort Walsh stockade. A mile downstream from the fort the creek bisects two old whiskey trading posts, which stand barely a hundred yards apart. This is where the Cypress Hills massacre took place a year before the Mounties came, when a party of wolfers and white whiskey traders fired on an Assiniboine camp in a field beside a muddy slough.

It is hard to imagine that such a peaceful place was the scene of such a murderous event. No one is sure now how many Indians were killed that day—many of them were women and children—but it was a brutal, unprovoked business, emblematic of the lawlessness of Canada's western prairie, and the urgency behind the Mounties' trek.

September 2nd, 1874—Wednesday
On the march at 7:30. Marched on till noon, had dinner and started off again at 2 p.m. Country very hilly crossing the Cypress Hills. A little excitement today. The advance guard killed five buffalo out of six that they came across. Two of them were brought into camp and served out as rations, allowing two pounds per man. One that Col. French shot weighed 950 lbs dressed. Had a good feed of buffalo liver. Fine weather.

It's high summer, just as it was a hundred and twenty seven years ago when James came this way. The ground falls away from the western edge of the Cypress Hills tableland to the plains. The distant horizon dissolves and re-forms in the heat

270

haze, like a moving ocean. The landscape in front of us is boundless and arid, and flat except for three small bumps far to the southwest, so faint in the distance that they're more of a suggestion than a fact. The Mounties called these hills the Three Buttes. They're known now as the Sweet Grass Hills, and they stand in northern Montana, close to the international boundary.

Down on the flatlands a lone tree lifts out of the heat, shivering like a spectre. A northern harrier sits up on a fence post, and watches a lithe, cloud-coloured coyote jog silently across wheat stubble, its grey-black ears alert for sounds. Red-tailed hawks float on the air currents, searching for small game. A porcupine lies dead at the side of the road.

In the night the air cracks and heaves with the dissipating heat of the day, fills the nostrils with warm scents, cleans them out again with sudden cool draughts.

September 5th, 1874—Saturday
On the march at daylight, very rough roads. Country very stony and hilly. Lots of choke berries. In going down a hill the back of one of my wagon wheels broke, and the driver (Chamberlain) was thrown out and barely escaped with his life. Camped about 6 p.m. at Milk River. A fine name for it as there is no water in it. One of my team horses played out. No grass. Weather fine.

But it wasn't the Milk River. It was more likely a branch of the South Saskatchewan, as the Mounties were miles to the north of where they thought they were. By now the scout Moreau had lost the confidence of Colonel French, who was beginning to believe that his scout was in the pay of the whiskey traders, and guiding them away from the forts.

271

The situation became serious. The Mounties spent the next two weeks wandering the southern Alberta prairie, lost and hungry, and increasingly demoralised, with winter approaching fast. James's diary is sprinkled with caustic comments.

September 6th, 1874—Sunday
Flour was reduced to ten oz. per man for the week. Baking powder was also reduced. Struck tents at 2:30 p.m. on account of no grass, and marched until dark . . .

September 9th—Wednesday
Eight horses died last night, so the camp was called Dead Horse Camp. The horses are getting played out fast. Three of B Troop boys went after water tonight and got lost, so they lay out all night. We are used to that sort of work and cold now.

September 11th—Friday
We are lost on the prairie. No one knows where we are. Council of the officers was held and decided to make for the Three Buttes on the Boundary Trail. Horses and oxen dying fast. Provisions getting scarce. Things look very dark. Weather very cold.

And so the force turned towards the south, to look for food and water at the Milk River and the Sweet Grass Hills. Colonel French was rapidly losing his authority with the officers and men.

The Milk River rises among the Rocky Mountains in eastern Montana, and climbs into Alberta before dipping down again below the border. Over the centuries it has carved its face into soft sandstone rock, and the twisting plains winds have added their own trickeries to the river canyon. Together the wind and the river have constructed monoliths, and what geologists call hoodoos. These contorted rocks and outcrops stand up like silent shamans, and watch over the waters that make their way down into the Missouri-Mississippi system, and on to the Gulf of Mexico.

The Milk River was given its name by the American explorers Lewis and Clark when they came upon it in 1805, because of the colour of its water. But the plains people—the Blackfoot and the Peigan and the Blood—called this steep-sided canyon Aysin'eep, or "Has Been Written" and it is a sacred place to them. For centuries their young men have come here on the vision quest, in search of the valley's magic, seeking knowledge of other dimensions.

We're camped in a thicket by the riverbank, among stunted cottonwood trees. Once this river valley was full of strong trees nurtured by the river, but the best of them have been taken down over the years for tipi poles, firewood, for more modern shelters and farm buildings.

Above the camp, the tops of the cliffs are sculpted stone, chiselled and flattened by the prairie winds, the sandstone worn into fantastic shapes, and riven with crannies where rattlesnakes live. Small purple plants hide among the hoodoos, and stunted junipers give out aromatic vapours.

Over the centuries, the native people have carved pieces of their history into the rock walls. Their ancient petroglyphs are delicate and spidery, elegantly simple and graphic, depicting skirmishes, shields and lances, and spiritual symbols; more recent etchings show horses and guns.

The day is hot, and a searing wind sweeps off the prairie. Children splash in the cool water at a slow curve in the river just off a sand beach, and ride rubber tubes and air mattresses under broken cliffs. These sandstone river cliffs are honeycombed with the homes of martins, which fly exquisitely upstream on crescent-shaped wings, skimming the surface of the water, collecting mosquitoes and sandflies.

A magpie stands on the front bumper of a truck, picking off dead flies with its beak. It flutters over to one of the campsites and alights on a table, starts to peck at the cellophane wrapping on a loaf of bread. A family of brown mule deer stands nervously at the edge of a patch of riverbank scrub, a buck and a doe and three fawns. The mother, with one foot raised, her ears moving with the shifting sounds, keeps herself between her offspring and the humans.

James and the wagons reached the Milk River valley long after the rest of B Troop. For some days they had been watched by groups of unseen Indians, who could make no sense of the Mounties' movements.

September 18th, 1874—Friday
We are in a beautiful ravine . . . Got up at daylight and roasted some meat. Made a cup of tea. Two horses dead. Marched two miles . . . passed three dead horses and came up to our Troop at 9 p.m. Camped in a ravine. Weather fine. Snow seen on the Three Buttes.

September 20th, 1874—Sunday
Our horse and ox both dead. Had dinner at Milk River, then marched three miles and came up to the whole force. Camped in a valley, the Butte Valley, a very beautiful place and rich in minerals. Coal, iron and alum in abundance. Had a splendid dinner today of antelope the scout shot; the last square meal I will likely have for some time. The boys christened the camp

Dead Horse Valley, as there were fifteen horses and four oxen died here. Weather fine.

Commissioner French took Colonel Macleod and a small party off to Fort Benton in Montana to buy supplies. He had determined that he would lead two troops back to Winnipeg when he returned, and leave the three remaining troops under Macleod's command, to deal with the question of frontier authority and fulfil the Mounties' original orders—to shut down the whiskey business and the traders' forts near present day Lethbridge. In essence, Commissioner French retired gracefully from the scene. Meanwhile the main body of the force slowly recovered their strength while they waited for Colonel Macleod to return from Fort Benton.

September 27th, 1874—Sunday
West Butte camp. Most of us washing our clothes. Washed my clothes and had to go in my drawers and no shirt until my clothes dried. If the people of Canada were to see us now with bare feet, not one half clothed; half starved, picking up fragments left by the American troops and hunting buffalo for meat, and have to pay for the ammunition used in killing them, I wonder what they would say of Colonel French . . . He left here with the best wishes of the men that he may never come back.

"I'm going over to the old Mountie post this evening," says the park ranger. "I've got to take some supplies there, a rifle and a couple of artefacts. You might find it interesting to come along." I've been talking to him about James.

The sun is dying as we walk down to the riverbank, but the air is warm, flitting with small insects. A shadow crosses my face as a grey owl swoops down the path, passes inches over my head without a sound, lights in a tree behind, watches motionless and observant. In that moment I find it possible to understand how a small animal would be transfixed in the presence of such absolute stealth.

The ranger's name is Matthew. He carries a long, twisted stick in his hand, a lever-action Winchester rifle slung over his shoulder. Fingers of dark shadow reach out from the canyon wall. Matthew lets himself down the bank, and steps into the slow river.

"Follow me carefully," he says, "stay right in my track." He prods the riverbed in front of him for holes as he moves slowly upstream, keeping parallel to the bank.

The water rises up past my thighs. The current tugs at me. Matthew pokes at the bank with his long stick. "Just in case," he says. "Sometimes there are rattlers here." He finds a thin gravel bar with his feet, and moves out towards the middle of the river, which is about a hundred feet wide at this place. The water eases up above my waist.

There's a serenity to all this—the river pulling at my legs like slow mercury, the warm evening air eddying past. Somewhere in the crossing of the river, time shifts with the subtle oscillation of a radio frequency, as if we're being moved back a hundred years. When we climb out on the south bank the silence is visceral, but for the soft sighing of the water, a wash of warm wind, and over by the cliffs, the kee-ing of a hawk.

"The Indians used to camp here long before the smugglers and the police came," says Matthew quietly, as we make our way through sagebrush towards the little police post. "There's always water and game at the mouths of the coulees. They could come and go without being seen, and they could hide war parties in the cuts. According to the Peigan, all the coulees between the Sweet Grass Hills and the Milk River were filled with Indian lodges in the fall of 1866, only a few years before the Mounties came through here." He taps a flat rock beside the front door of the cabin with his stick, checking again for rattlesnakes.

The old police post is a sturdy structure of split logs and boards, the wood whitewashed to protect it from the weather, a shake roof on top. A small stable stands a few yards away. The original steading was built fifteen years after James passed this way with the first Mounties. This building is a more recent construction, but built to the original plans, and placed on the old foundation stones.

It's tidy and snug inside, with extra blankets folded at the foot of neatly made beds, and spare tunics hanging from pegs, as if the Mounties have just gone out on patrol. An oiled, topographical map of Assiniboia—the old name for the prairie territories—fills the wall above a desk, a set of scales to one side. Sepia-tinged photographs hang beside one of the beds; a buffalo skull watches from a chest by the window. A pot-bellied stove stands in the middle of the floor, and a heavy buffalo-hide coat lies across a chair, waiting for the snows. In the kitchen, a scrubbed wooden table is set with cutlery and crockery for four, with an oil lamp in its centre. Matthew lifts a trapdoor in the floor to reveal a dank, earthen root cellar. "They used to put prisoners down here," he says. "It can't have been very nice; sometimes we find rattlers in it." A cord of winter wood is stacked neatly at the back door.

October 2nd, 1874—Friday
Camped on Milk River. The riverbanks are lined with buffaloes, there must be at least ten or fifteen thousand. The largest herd we have seen. Weather fine. Country sandy.

The ranger, Matthew, takes us up the coulee behind the police post. This canyon cuts deep into the flat prairie for miles, back across the US border, all the way to the base of the Sweet Grass Hills. It was a prime route for the American whiskey traders, for they could stay hidden in its confines until they were far inside Canada.

"The smugglers called it Police Coulee," says Matthew. He indicates a steep track which cuts up the side and disappears over the rim of the coulee towards the border town of Coutts, ten miles away. Then he points out a rock with signatures etched across its face.

"Some of the Mounties who were posted here found the life very hard. Once the post was established no self-respecting smuggler would come this way, so there was little for the Mounties to do. At one time or another the fellows who were posted here would come up to this rock and carve their names on it. Most of them were bored out of their minds, and unfortunately some of them took to drink."

October 3rd—Saturday
Being in a stationary camp there is not much to do. On buffalo chips fatigue for our mess cook, and in the afternoon out skinning and cutting up two buffaloes. Robinson of F Troop blew off one of his fingers by a shotgun bursting. Weather a little cold.

Late on a hot summer afternoon, Em and I drive across the border, past the dusty little towns of Sweetgrass and Sunburst, and turn off on a dirt road towards the southern base of the Sweet Grass Hills. The road is narrow and poorly maintained, with broken tarmac—little more than a farm

278

track. Cattle are scattered across the green slopes, standing, watching, chewing patiently. A group of smart quarter horses looks sleek and healthy, ready to work.

These gentle hills rise up from the prairie like islands, sidestepped millennia ago by the ice sheets which levelled the land around them. Montana grassland rolls away on every side, opening out immense vistas of land and sky and space, like a suspension in time. A weathered scree face looks volcanic; a tuft of trees grows at its side. In a shift of the summer light the hills look for a moment startlingly familiar, like the Scottish border hills; as if they could have been visited by Picts and Romans, as if stone age forts might have been constructed on their tops, and ancient quarries established up there to supply the hunters of the plains with arrowheads and lance points.

October 6th—Tuesday
It is just one year today since I listed. Then I was in Toronto; now I am on guard on the prairie, a long way from home.

October 7th, 1874—Wednesday
A party of traders passed our camp who were duly searched. No liquor found. We clubbed together and bought 100 lbs of flour from them for twelve dollars and a five gallon keg of syrup for twelve dollars. Going to have a blow out tonight. Weather fine. Beautiful sight of the Rocky Mountains, the peaks are all covered with snow.

Towards the middle of the month the Mounties move north to a place called Slippery Springs, not far from present day Lethbridge. James explains that the name came about because a small party of traders were once attacked here by

279

a group of Indians. The man on guard was wearing carpet slippers, and lost one of them in the fight.

October 15th, 1874—Thursday
On the move at sunrise, passed the skeleton of an Indian. Crossed the St. Mary's River. Upset one of our wagons in going up the hill after crossing the river.

October 16th—Friday
Up at sunrise loading up the wagon that upset. On the move at 8 a.m. Weather fine, air smoky. Prairie on fire.

A rust-coloured sun sinks slowly into the dark peaks behind Head-Smashed-in-Buffalo-Jump in the Porcupine Hills, the rolling foothills of the Rockies, on the rim of the western prairie. A single horizontal cloud balances in the sky like a delicate silver feather.

We've come to get a good view of the country where James ended his journey. The Blackfoot lived up here, and drove the wild buffalo to their deaths over these scarp cliffs in elaborately prepared, ritualised hunts. They used every part of the animal for food, medicine, clothing, shelter, and weapons.

From the top of these weathered cliffs we can see far over southern Alberta, observe the patterns of the rivers, and select likely crossing places. On this warm summer evening the land below lies green and nourished between its brown horizons, and we can pick out the places where the Mounties might have found water, and game to eat.

All of it is Alberta cattle country now, and the buffalo plains are spread with small farms, edged by rule-straight dirt roads and tidy fences. A hawk cries in the distance, and a harvest moon rises up behind hydro wires that hum with electricity.

October 17th, 1874—Saturday

On the move at sunrise. Marched eight miles when we halted for breakfast on the Belly River. There was an alarm in camp about Indians when two of the boys went out and fetched in four Blood Indians. Had a shake hands all round and gave them some grub. After breakfast we crossed the Belly River and moved about ten miles and camped. Dry camp, but we had water in our barrels.

With winter coming up hard, the Mounties built a fort on an island in the Oldman River and named it after Assistant Commissioner Macleod. But in time the fort was damaged by spring floods, and so it was abandoned and rebuilt on the riverbank a short distance away. It stands now in the centre of a busy Alberta township, with a refurbished stockade and bastions, souvenir stores and flush toilets—an important tourist attraction.

October 18th, 1874—Sunday

On the move at sunrise. Marched five miles when we came up to the rest of the boys camped on an island on the Old Man's River. The boys are raising quite a row among the whiskey traders having captured an outfit, spilt all the whiskey, confiscated one hundred and sixty buffalo robes, and fined them seven hundred dollars. The M. Police boys are beginning to do business. The command arrived here October 13th. Our tramping is over for this summer.

Epilogue: The Milk River

This strange valley is timeless, and strong with its spirits. It's an elemental place, satiated with life and death, the river running through it like a thread, on its long way across the continent from the mountains to the sea, as it has done through the ages—past war and pestilence, oblivious to the trials of man.

Changing weathers scour the planet around this valley, and turn and shape our landscapes. Political winds blow hot and cold, left and right, liberal, conservative—and ordinary people are caught up in the forces they generate, too often powerless to influence the changes that occur.

It's clear to me, as I stand on these weathered sandstone cliffs, that the greatest questions we have are not only about survival and sustenance; that they cannot just be wrapped up neat and tidy, and finished with. They're not just about roots either, because we all inhabit this planet together. No, the questions of life are also about change and altered states, about nature and experience, about curiosity and questioning, and understanding.

Over that empty horizon lies a modern state that, in little more than a hundred years, has made an enormous leap from its natural condition. It's hard to understand the speed of this change, difficult to imagine the scale of what has been lost—hard to balance that against what might have been gained. I was imprinted by Europe's oldest cultures, raised in one of its ancient cities, where the centuries still show across its customs and its speech, and lie layered through its architecture. But here, in little more than a hundred years, this country has transformed from wild prairie and primeval forest to modern towns and cities, raced to the forefront of the most advanced technologies. It has been a journey far beyond the imaginings of my relative James Finlayson, and it has rarely carried with it the underpinning knowledge of the people who understood the spirit of this land, its secrets and its gods. Young Blackfoot have been coming here in search of spiritual understanding for more than three thousand years—seeking revelations, gathering talismans for their medicine pipe bundles, their beaver bundles, their Sun Dance bundles. Their parents hunted here, held gatherings and festivals, told stories, had sport, wrote tales on the riverworn cliffs. It is difficult to believe that our modern society would not have been richer by encompassing the learning of these people, who were here so long before the conquering European cultures came.

As the fox said to St. Exupery's Little Prince: "What is essential is invisible to the eye . . ."

The air is cool and still. A pillar of smoke rises from a campfire down at the river bend. Across the plains the Sweet Grass Hills are printed sharply onto the southern skyline, changing colour as dusk sweeps across the plains: the Sweetgrass Hills, another site of great spiritual importance to the prairie peoples—the Blackfoot, the Cree, the Gros Ventre, the Sioux, and the Assiniboine.

It has taken me a long time to realise that Canada is where I live now; that this is a place where I feel comfortable and at home; that I've become like the people here. It's a good country this, a good place to travel from, a good place to return to. But I still belong to Scotland. It is still the only place on earth where I'm completely in tune with the landscape, where I am as much a part of it as the hills and the schist and the granite rocks. In Scotland I think like a Scot, in Canada like a North American. I contemplate this sometimes when my accent slides across the Atlantic Ocean, if it starts to thicken after a pint of beer, or a dram of whisky.

I used to wonder if that was a sign of a weak character. But I don't believe that any more. Now I know that I just belong to two countries.

Glossary

Blackies: Blackface sheep
Machair: low-lying, sand-based grassland, by the seashore.
Haugh: a Scots word meaning the low-lying land beside a river.
Drystane dyke: a stone wall built without the use of cement.
Kirk: Church
Conventicle: Religious assembly outside the auspices of the Church of England, outlawed by the Conventicle Act of 1664
Picquet: Guard duty
Bull train: Supply wagons
Wolfers: Hunters who lived by poisoning wolves and selling their hides. Hated by the Indians because their dogs often ate the poisoned meat.
Dinner: Lunch (mid-day)
Supper: Dinner (evening)

Acknowledgements

Sollas, and Encounter with the Bonxies have been published in Celtic Heritage, Halifax, Nova Scotia.

There are many people to thank.

First of all, for help with the writing and editing, my wife Marilyn Bowering—for taking the time to go over the pieces, and the whole, many times, and for her gentleness and tact. I know it wasn't easy. Most of all, for living with me in the magic glen and everywhere else, and for surviving for a year without central heating or telephones, and with an oven with a hole in it.

Thank you to Doug Beardsley for looking over an early draft, and offering me helpful strategic advice.

Thanks are also due for the content of the book, for all their help to me, and for the teachings and experiences without which life would be dull, to:

Glynn for telling me about the Island, and for opening my eyes.

The late John Lawrence of Duncan and Quamichan Lake for his great humanity and generosity . . . an endlessly decent man.

Horst Padur from the Mill—himself an immigrant, who began to show me the ways of Canadians.

The late Fred Reder, who took me on as a deckhand when I was an itinerant student, and introduced me to life on small boats on the high seas.

Pete Songhurst, for selling me the lemon-yellow Chevy for a hundred bucks; a sturdy old sled which took me up and down and across the west for years.

Buffy York and Brian McEneny and Mike Mezzner; thanks to Megg Loomis, Sandy Levitt, Bill Hutchison, Doug Taylor, Tom Gerber, Phil Carnahan, Anselm Baud, and everyone else who was patient with me at Mt. Hood. To cousin John Pittar in New Zealand, for stretching me to the limit, and beyond. And later to Doug and Rhoda Swanson, Gerry Carr, Genny Dark and Ken Brown.

Steve Lancaster in Santa Monica and his cousin Pete, for collecting me off the street one dark night and giving me a room and a home, without asking questions.

To Edie Gilien in Los Angeles, who used to sing with Cisco Houston, and who fed me when I was hungry.

To Helène from Johanneshov, near Stockholm, for so many things—but particularly for helping me to be strong at a time of discovery, for being the best hitch-hiking companion I could have had, for helping me find my way around Greenwich Village . . . and for introducing me to the music of Phil Ochs. To Helène's friends, Geza and Marion, who lived in Queens, New York. And to Danny, wherever you are.

Mum, for showing me my native land when I was young, and for joining me to it in inexpressible ways of the spirit. And for just about everything else.

Dochie, for giving us Solon, and to Rob and Betty Cairns for their surpassing Highland generosity, and for sharing some of the glen's secrets with us.

The late Bob Bissett, for introducing us to the mysteries of Breadalbane, and for telling us things that would otherwise have been unknowable.

Dad, for sharing firesides and beer and wonderful stories with me, and for linking past things to the present.

Phil Foster, for helping me to stay alive in the Scottish mountains, and Les Brettle, Faz Faraday, Colin Cruikshank, Angela Mortimer, Alan Chainey, Hetty Mustard, Janet Livingstone and the late Laurie Liddell.

The late Ken Latta of Sleat on Skye, and to Georgie at the Point.

Winspur, for creating great adventures, and to Ingrid for putting up with him, and for listening to the stories again from time to time when I turn up.

David Finlayson, and his late wife Angela, in Kingsbarns, for introducing me to parts of my family's history that I didn't know, and for the tales that accompanied it.

Iain Clarke in Evanton, and Maggie MacDonald in Dingwall, and to Emma and Ian and Wayne and Jerry at Albanet for their kindness and hospitality, and for their company at the Mallard.

Jack and Joe and Betty and Vivian for White Fish Lake: to Xan and Jessica for helping to bring Writing on Stone alive, albeit in different ways, but probably ways that great, grand-uncle James would have liked. And to Matthew

McHugh for introducing a sliver of magic into an unforgettable evening by the Milk River.

It occurs to me that I should also make apologies to the late Theodore Roethke for the last line of the piece entitled "Sollas".

I must also thank Tommy, from Edinburgh, Paris, and Beaumont-en-Auge in Normandy, for showing me how to see the place where I live as exotic, and those familiar things around me as different, even unique.

Finally, while the faults in this book are all mine, such virtues as it has would not exist without the guidance and patient editing of Hiro Boga and Ron Smith of Oolichan Books. Thank you.

Bibliography & References

1. Robert Louis Stevenson, *The Amateur Immigrant*. London: Hogarth Press, 1984.
2. Roger Duhamel, FRSC, *destination—CANADA*. Ottawa: Queen's Printer and Controller of Stationery, 1964. Cat. no. Ci 61-1864.
3. Marilyn Bowering, *Sleeping With Lambs*. Victoria & Toronto: Press Porcepic, 1980.
4. William A. Gillies, *In Famed Breadalbane*. Strathtay: Clunie Press, 1980.
5. John Prebble, *Glencoe*. London: Secker and Warburg, 1966.
6. WH Murray, *Mountaineering in Scotland*. London: Diadem Books, 1992.
7. A.R.B. Haldane, *The Drove Roads of Scotland*. Edinburgh: Birlinn Ltd., 1997.
8. John Marius Wilson, Ed., *The Imperial Gazetteer of Scotland, Volume II*. Edinburgh: A. Fullerton & Co., 1868.

9. *Jottings on the March: The Diary of Trooper James Finlayson*. Ottawa: National Archives, 1874. *

10. Sir Cecil B. Denny, *March of the Mounties*. Surrey, BC: Heritage House Publishing Company Ltd., 1994.

11. Jim Wallace, *A Double Duty*. Winnipeg: Bunker to Bunker Books, 1997.

12. David Cruise & Alison Griffiths, *The Great Adventure*. Toronto: Penguin Books Canada Ltd., 1996.

* Note: James Finlayson's diary is a contemporary record of an important event in Canadian history—the first major operation of the country's famous national police force. Trooper Finlayson's record was kept, not by a leader of the expedition with a natural disposition to show its successful achievement, but by a "ranker" who saw the expedition in its weakness, as well as its successes. As such it provides a degree of modification to the official story. It also places on record many minor aspects of the trek without affecting its major accomplishments, and helps to make it live as a contemporary social record. Trooper Finlayson's diary can claim to be of some genuine historic value.

Photo Credit: Marilyn Bowering

Michael Elcock was born in Forres, Scotland and grew up in Edinburgh and West Africa. He emigrated to Canada when he was twenty-one and worked in pulp mills, in the woods, on west coast fishing boats and as a ski instructor. Along the way he earned a B.A. and M.Ed. at the University of Victoria, and did post-graduate studies in Quebec, Sweden, Germany, Belgium and Scotland. He was Athletic Director at the University of Victoria for ten years, and then CEO of Tourism Victoria for five. In 1990 he moved with his wife and daughter to Andalusia to work on developing Spain's Expo '92. He now lives in Sooke, BC.

RECENT OOLICHAN TITLES

The Blue Sky • Galsan Tschinag

"With this novel, a Mongolian shaman has stepped onto the stage of world literature."—*Der Spiegel*

Elliot & Me • Keith Harrison

"The writing is beautiful and subtle and to me very poetic."
—Marilyn Bowering

Silent Inlet • Joanna Streetly

"A great book to curl up in a corner with . . . I loved it."
—Phyllis Reeve

Love In A Time of Terror • Ulla Berkéwicz

". . . meticulously observes reality and yet reaches beyond . . . into imagination and memory and the many layers of consciousness."
—Urs Bugmann

The School at Chartres • David Manicom

". . . a beautiful meditation on the many faces of love . . "
—*Montreal Review of Books*

Islands West: Stories from the Coast • Keith Harrison, ed.

" . . . a book you may return to again and again to ponder our precarious perch by the edge of the sea." —Vivian Moreau, *Times Colonist*

To view our complete catalogue, visit us online at
www.oolichan.com